EVERYDAY SEWING

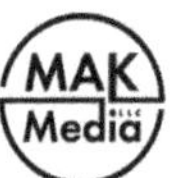

Published by MAK Media LLC

2nd edition June 2021

ISBN
Paperback: 978-1-955721-14-1

EVERYDAY SEWING

SIMPLE PATTERNS & SEWING TUTORIALS

Maria Ragone

Table of Contents

Introduction

I am excited to share with you some of my favorite everyday patterns! To use this book simply cut the patterns out or trace them with tracing paper. Each product is customizable and giftable.

Have fun sewing!

Bib Pattern

Materials:
-Base fabric
-Waterproof Lining fabric
-1″ x 1.5″ / 25mm x 38mm hook and loop tape

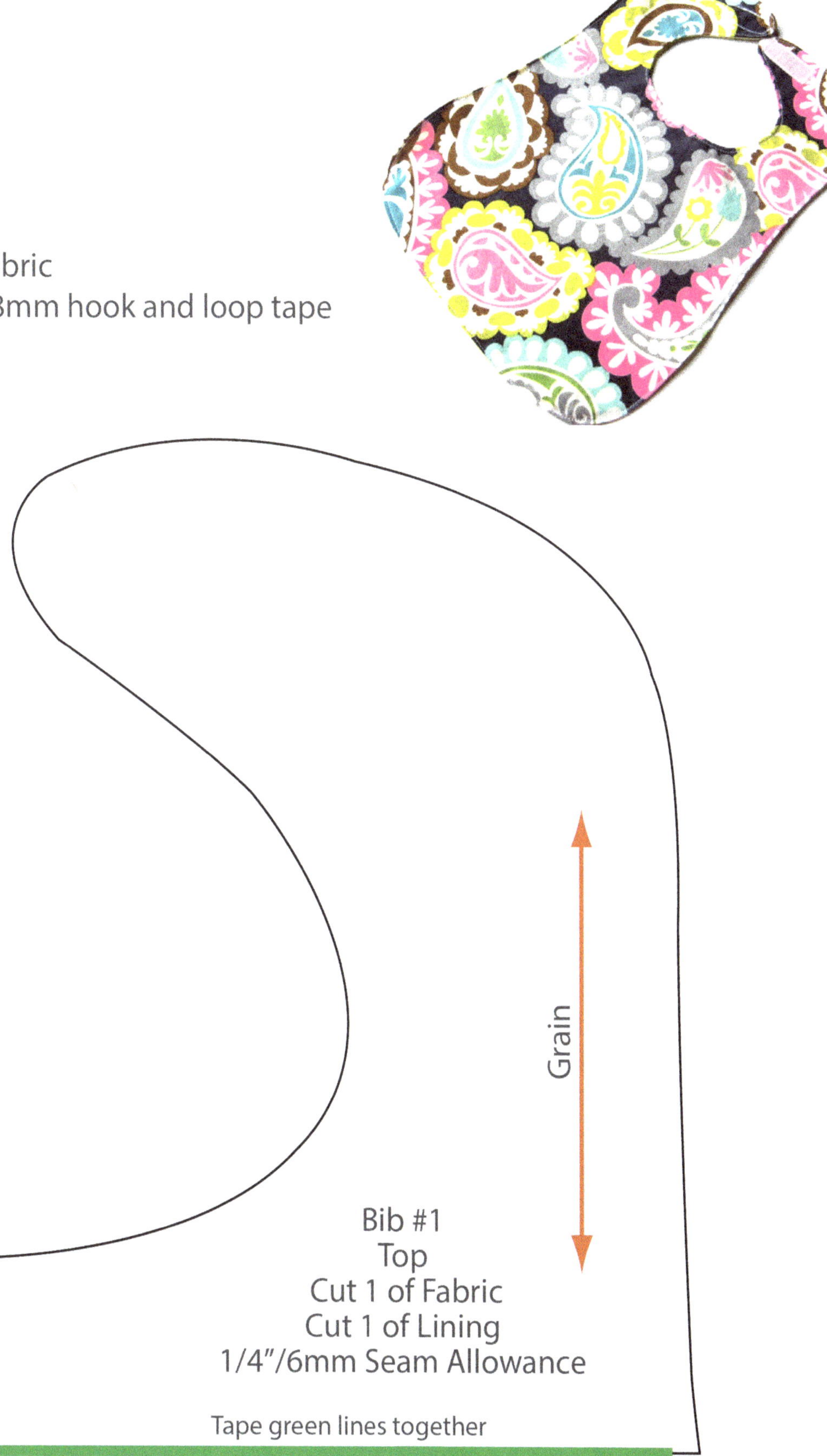

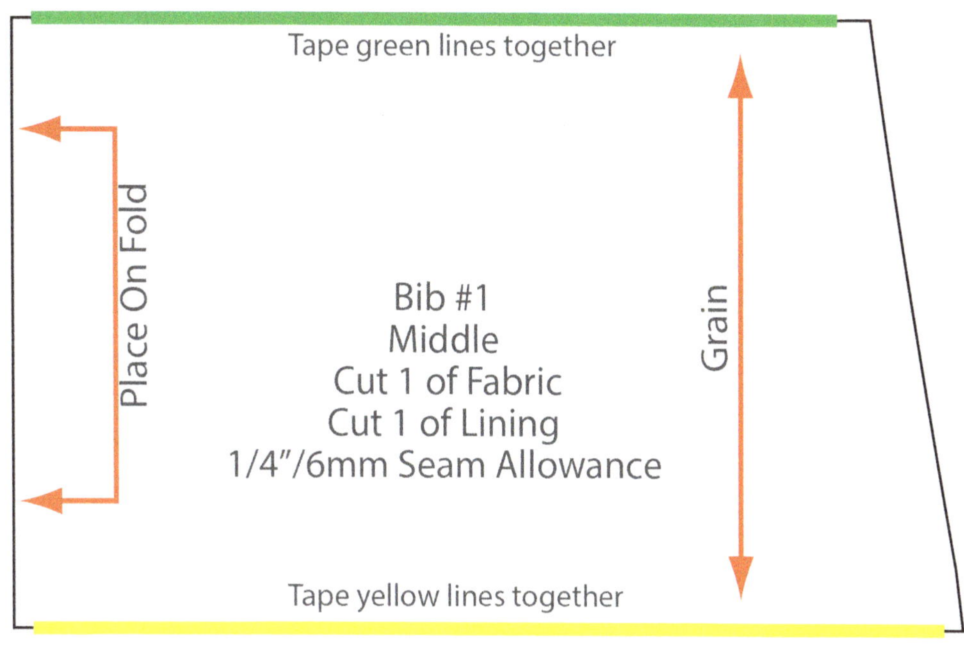
Tape green lines together
Place On Fold
Bib #1
Middle
Cut 1 of Fabric
Cut 1 of Lining
1/4"/6mm Seam Allowance
Grain
Tape yellow lines together

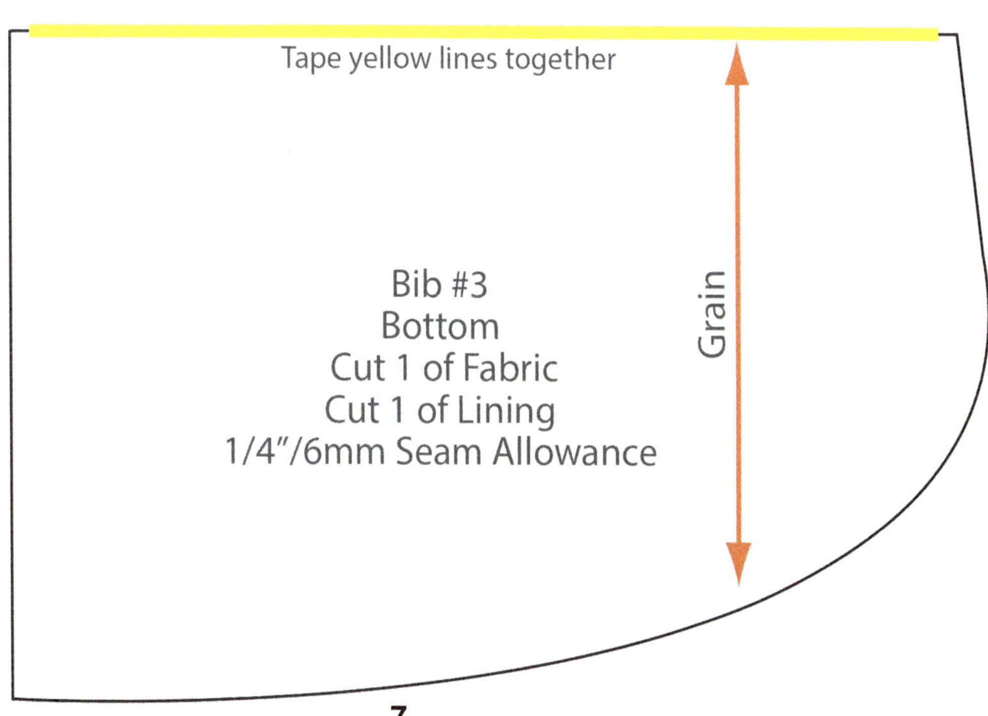
Tape yellow lines together
Bib #3
Bottom
Cut 1 of Fabric
Cut 1 of Lining
1/4"/6mm Seam Allowance
Grain

Bib Tutorial

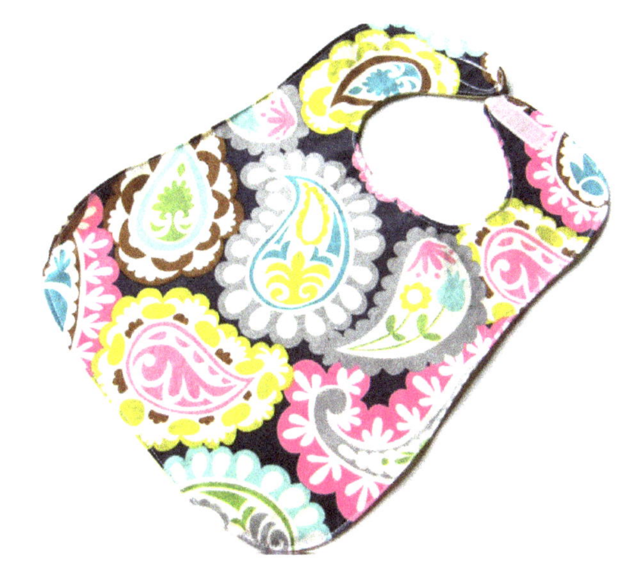

Materials:
-Base fabric
-Waterproof Lining fabric
-1″ x 1.5″ / 25mm x 38mm hook and loop tape

Step 1

-Cut out the patterns.
Be sure to select "do not scale" in your printer settings.

-If you are making a solid fabric bib tape together yellow and green lines.
-If you are making a 3 panel bib do not tape.

***Only one half of the bib is provided you can either print 2 copies of the bib halves and tape together, or place the middle line on the fold of the fabric to cut out one solid bib.

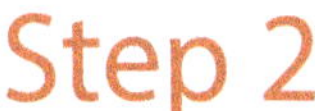

Step 2

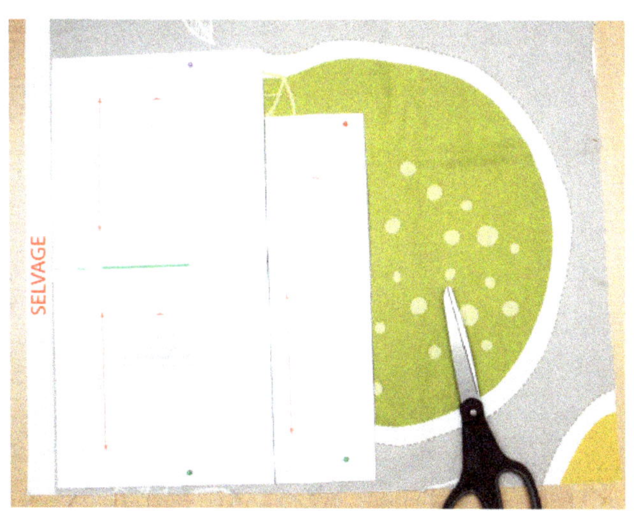

-Position the pattern pieces on the fabric so the grain line runs parallel to the grain or selvage of the fabric. (If you have directional fabric as shown in photo with a clear top and bottom to the design place the grain line parallel to the design).

-Mark all notches, lines and dots on the fabric

Step 3

-If you are making a solid fabric bib skip to step 5

-Sew the pieces together with right sides together match appropriate seams

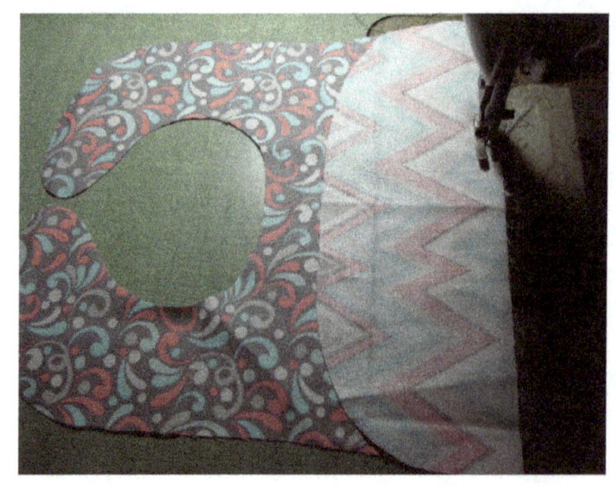

Step 4

-Iron the seams open

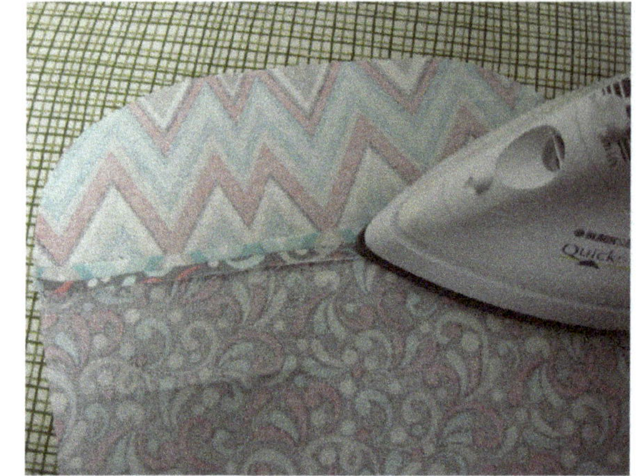

Step 5

-Place right sides of bib and waterproof lining together. (If applicable right side of waterproof linin is the shiney wipeable side)

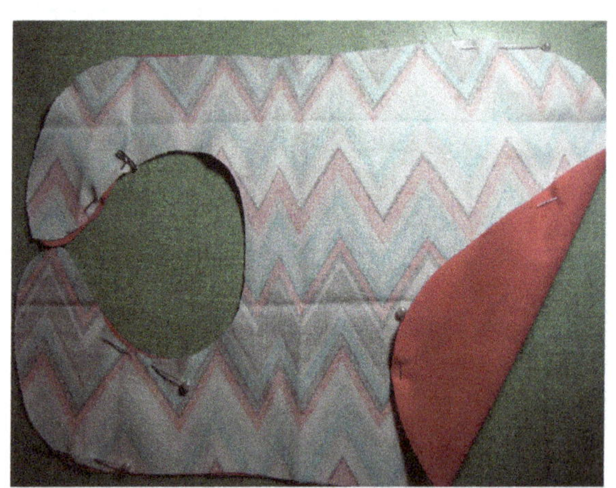

-Sew around the perimeter of the bib starting at the bottom notch

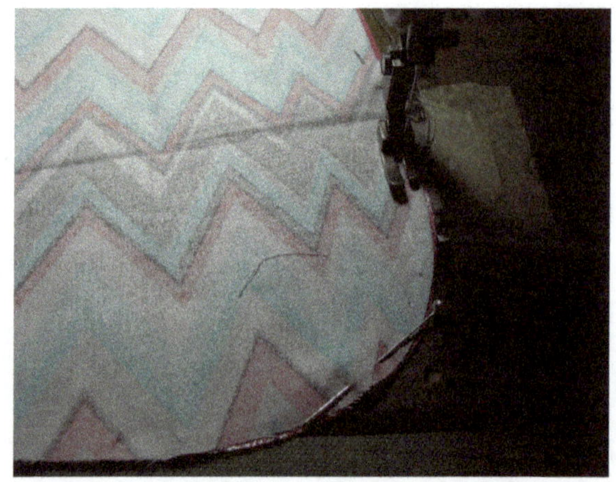

Step 6

-Leave an opening at the bottom

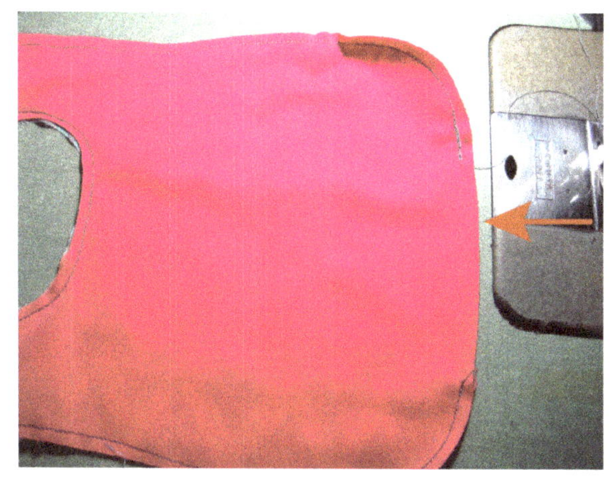

-Trim seam allowance around all curves leaving scant edge (don't trim too close; you don't want to break the seam)

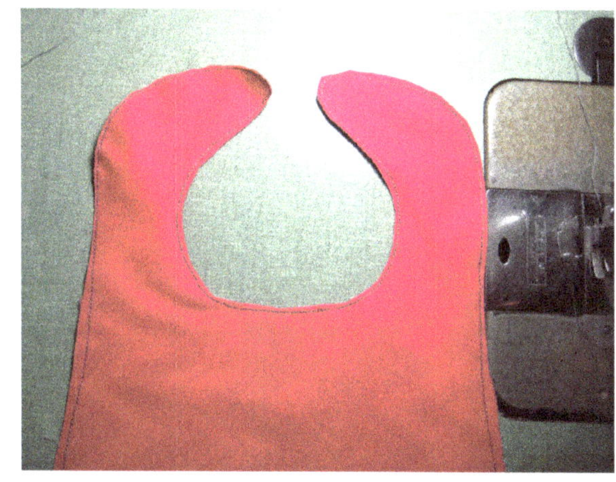

Step 7

-Turn bib right sideout

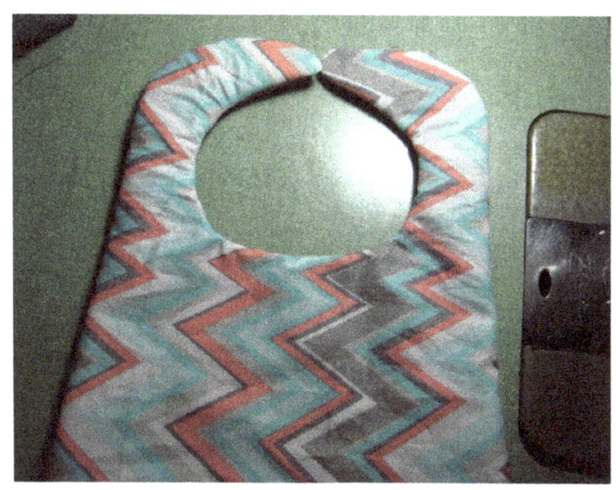

-Iron flat with bottom seam allowance folded in (don't melt the waterproof fabric)

-Pin bottom seam

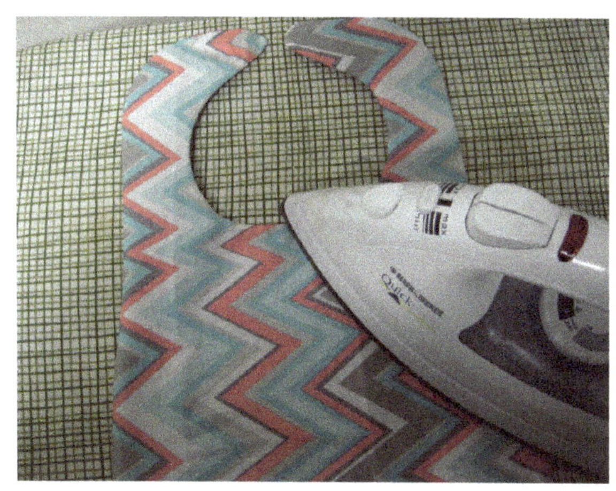

Step 8

-Top stitch along entire perimeter of bib

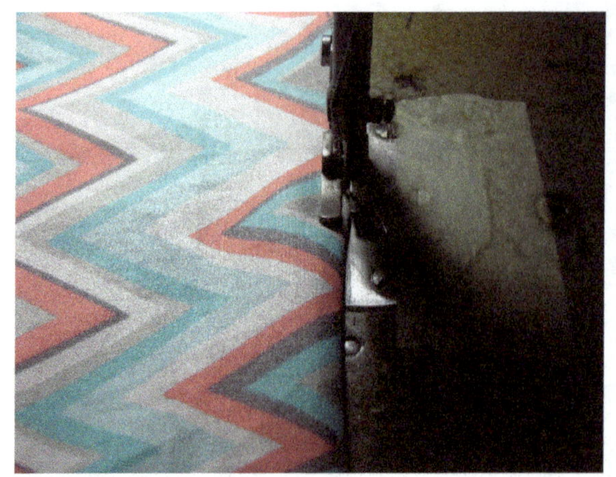

Step 9

-Attach hook and loop tape

-Cut the tape ends to round of the corners (loop tape should be longer to allow for tightening adjustments on baby)

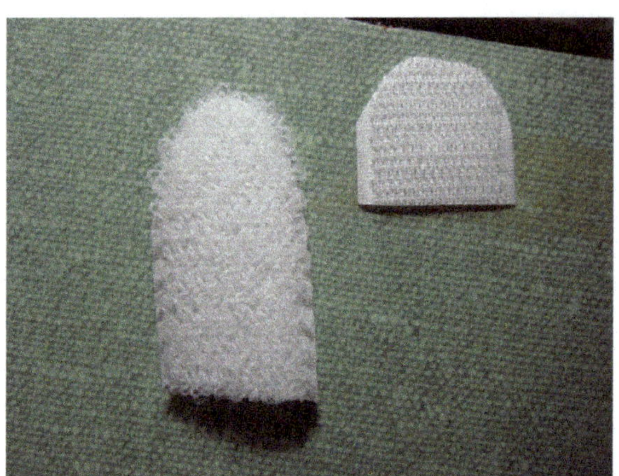

-Be sure to attach hook tape on right side/front of bib so it won't scratch baby's skin.

-Top stitch around perimeter of tape

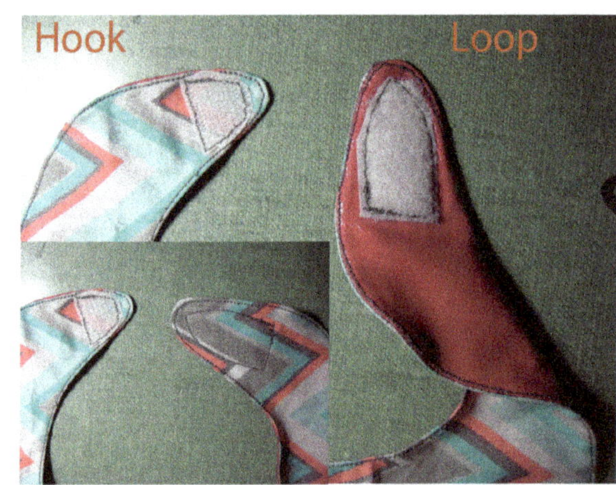

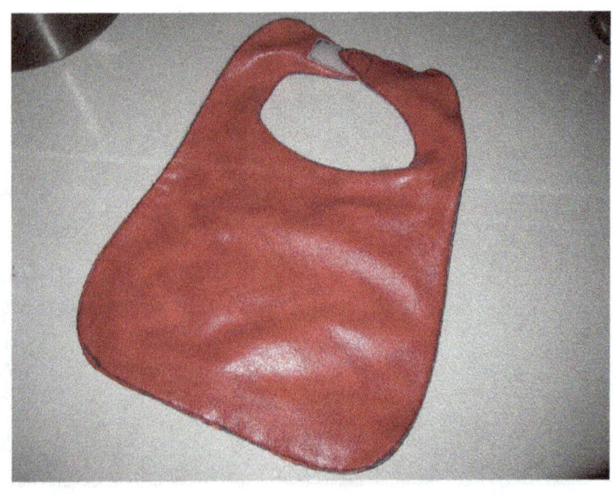

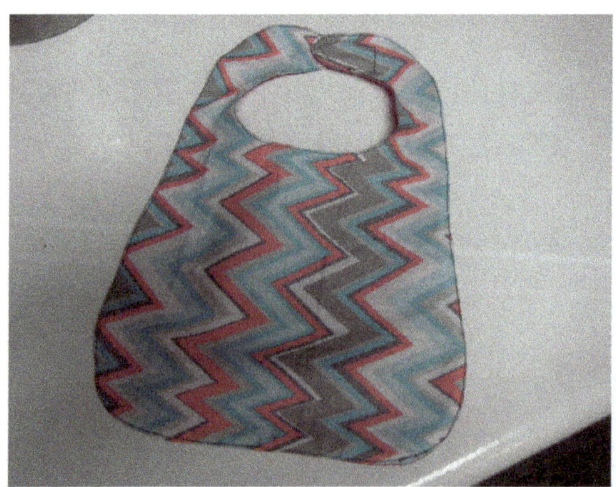

Cosmetic Bag Pattern

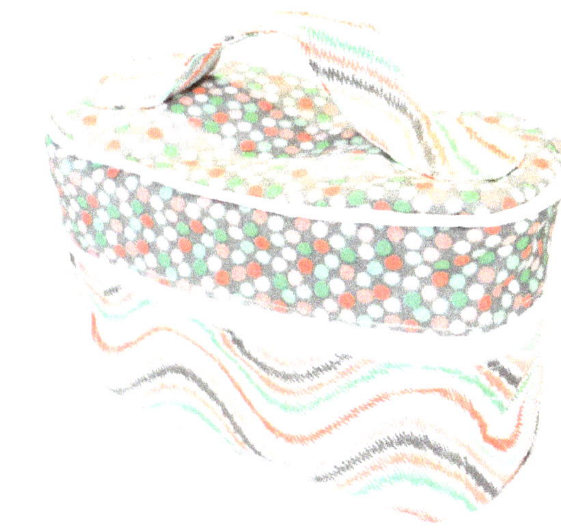

Grain

Cosmetic Bag #1
Back
Cut 1 of Fabric A
Cut 1 of Lining
1/4"/6mm Seam Allowance
Piece Dimensions: 4" x 5" / 10.2cm x 12.7cm

Cosmetic Bag #2
Back
Cut 1 of Fusible Fleece
Piece Dimensions: 3.5" x 3.25" / 8.9cm x 8.3cm

Cosmetic Bag #10
Top/Bottom Interior
Cut 2 of Ultra Firm Stabilizer
Cut 2 of Fusible Fleece
1/4"/6mm Seam Allowance

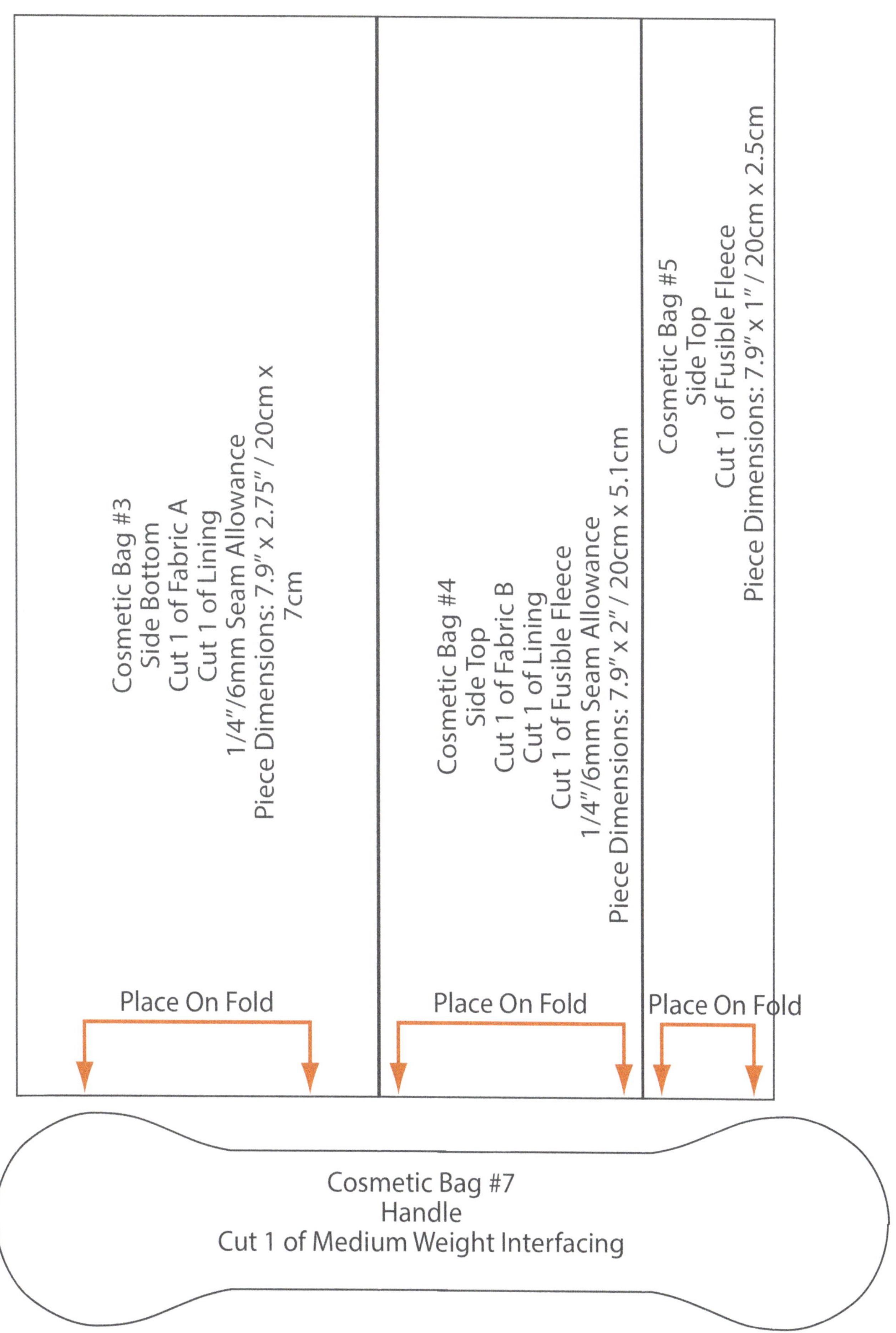
Cosmetic Bag #3
Side Bottom
Cut 1 of Fabric A
Cut 1 of Lining
1/4"/6mm Seam Allowance
Piece Dimensions: 7.9" x 2.75" / 20cm x 7cm
Place On Fold
Cosmetic Bag #4
Side Top
Cut 1 of Fabric B
Cut 1 of Lining
Cut 1 of Fusible Fleece
1/4"/6mm Seam Allowance
Piece Dimensions: 7.9" x 2" / 20cm x 5.1cm
Place On Fold
Cosmetic Bag #5
Side Top
Cut 1 of Fusible Fleece
Piece Dimensions: 7.9" x 1" / 20cm x 2.5cm
Place On Fold
Cosmetic Bag #7
Handle
Cut 1 of Medium Weight Interfacing

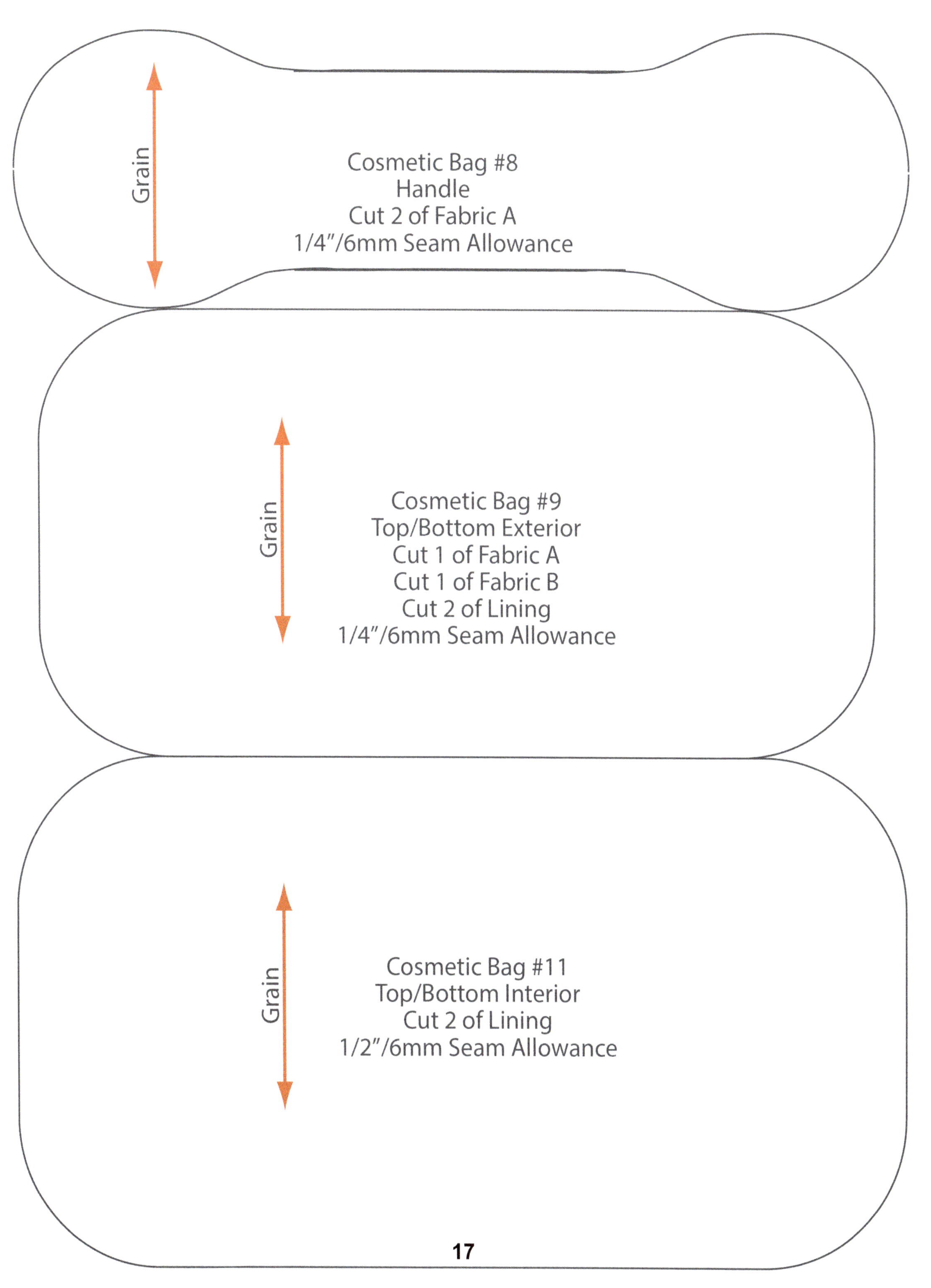
Grain
Cosmetic Bag #8
Handle
Cut 2 of Fabric A
1/4"/6mm Seam Allowance
Grain
Cosmetic Bag #9
Top/Bottom Exterior
Cut 1 of Fabric A
Cut 1 of Fabric B
Cut 2 of Lining
1/4"/6mm Seam Allowance
Grain
Cosmetic Bag #11
Top/Bottom Interior
Cut 2 of Lining
1/2"/6mm Seam Allowance

Cosmetic Bag Tutorial

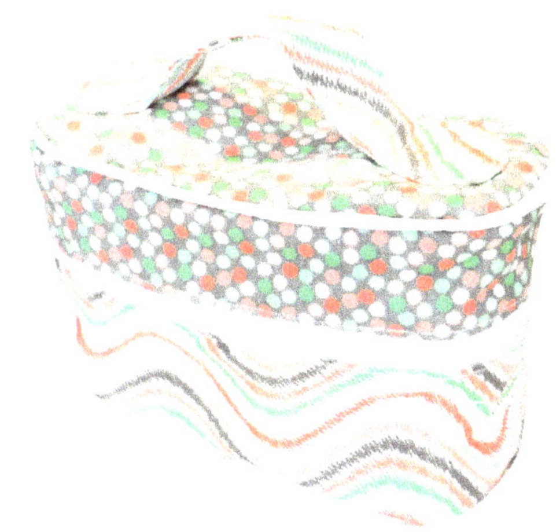

Materials:
- 1/4 yd/m cotton fabric A
- 1/4 yd/m cotton fabric B
- 1/4 yd/m cotton or waterproof lining fabric
- 1/4 yd/m fusible fleece
- 8″ x 8“ / 21cm x 21cm ultra firm stabilizer
- 6″ x 2“ / 16cm x 5cm medium weight interfacing
- 17″ zipper
- 1 yd/m of 1/4″ / 6mm piping
- Ruler
- Pencil
- Sewing machine
- Iron
- Thread

Step 1

-Prewash and pre-iron cotton fabrics.

-Print and cut out the patterns.
Be sure to select "do not scale" in your printer settings.

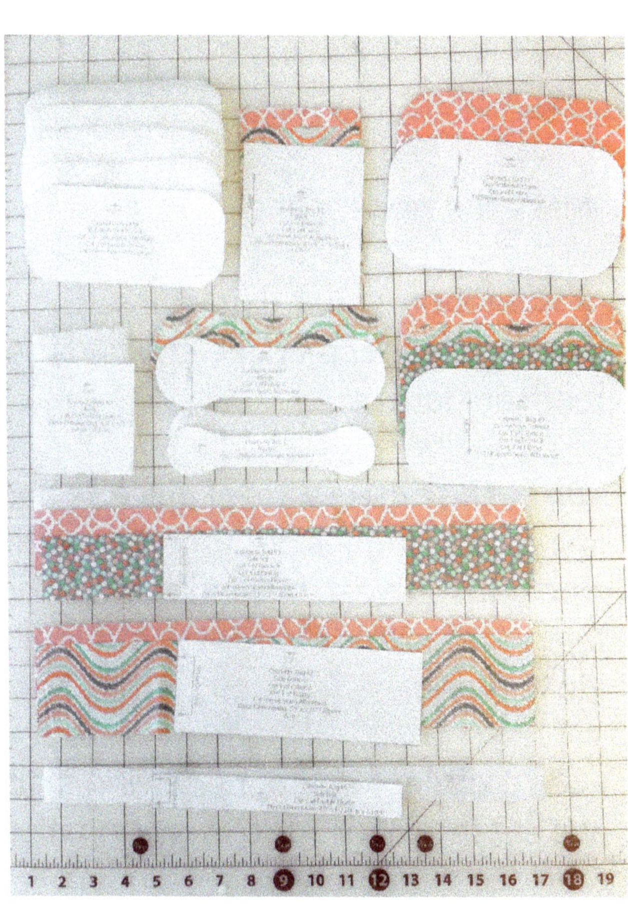

Step 2

-Position the pattern pieces on the fabric so the grain lines run parallel to the grain or selvage of the fabric. (If you have directional with a clear top and bottom to the design place the grain line parallel to the design).

Step 3

-Iron the fusible fleeece onto the center of the wrong side of fabric of pieces #1, #3, #4, & #8 according to the manufacturer's instructions (note: skinny strip of fleece #5 to be ironed to skinny cotton piece #4).

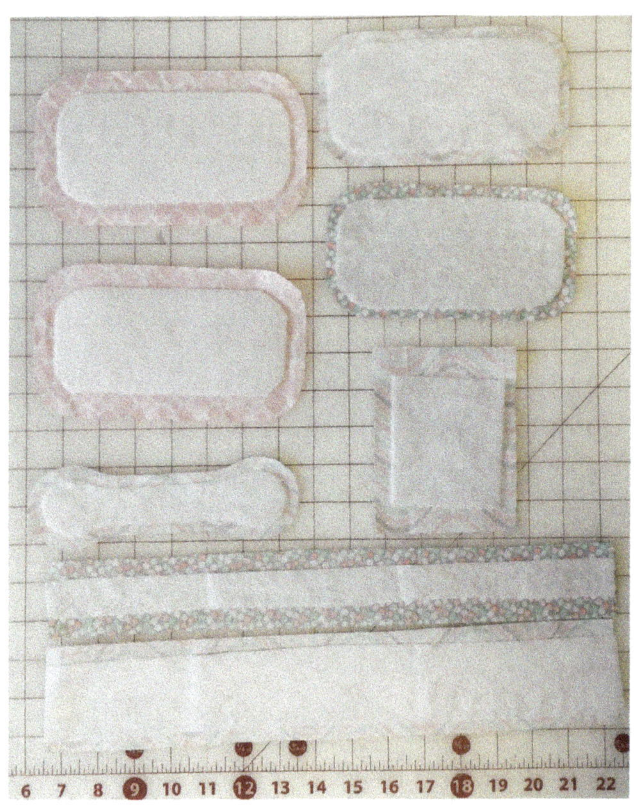

-Iron the stabilizer onto the center of the wrong side of fabric of piece #11 according to the manufacturer's instructions.

Step 4

-Make the zipper panels

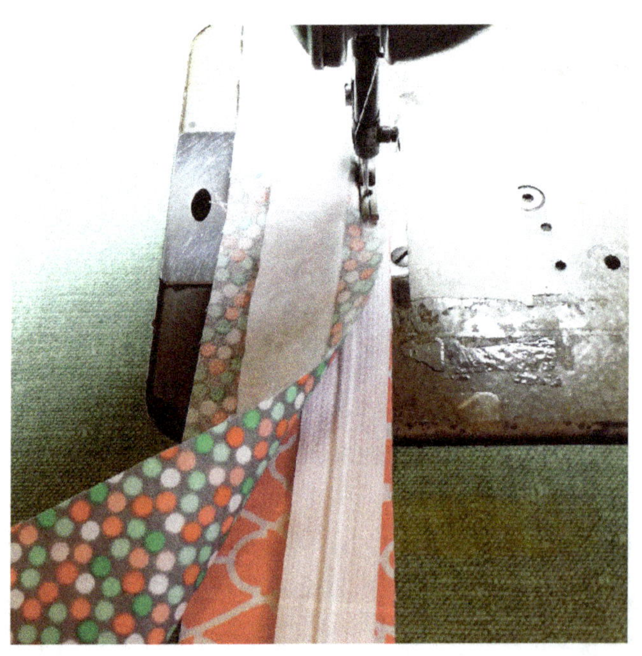

-Position the zipper so it is closed, the zipper slider is at one end and the teeth are facing up.

- Place the outer fabric of piece #4 and lining fabric right sides together with the zipper in between making sure the zipper teeth are facing towards the outer fabric. Pin in place.

- Use a zipper foot on the sewing machine and stitch 1/8" or 3mm away from the teeth.

Step 5

-Flip both fabrics so wrong sides are together and top stitch along the seam near the zipper teeth.

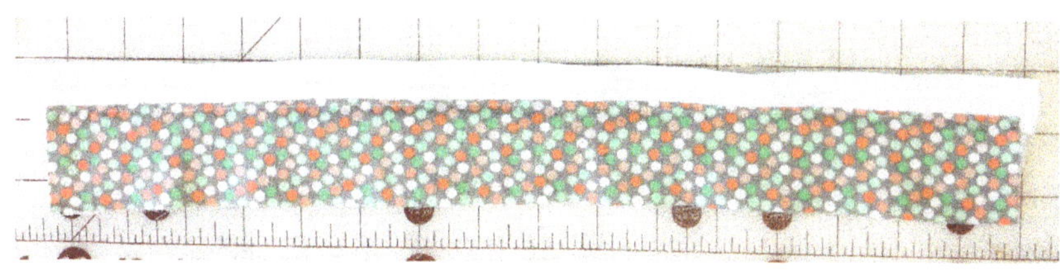

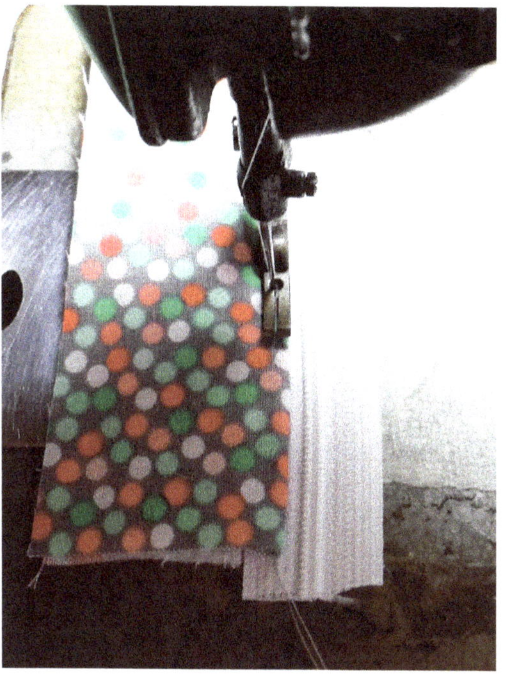

Step 6

-Repeat steps 4 & 5 for piece #3 to complete the zipper panels

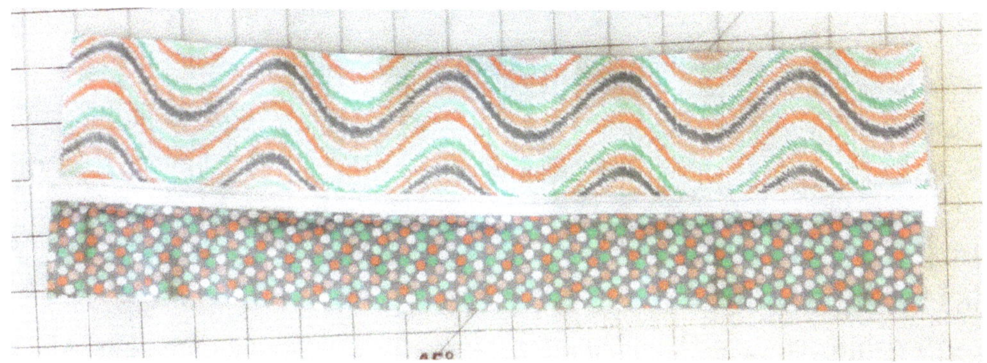

Step 7

-Trim off sides to measure 15.25" / 38.7cm long.

-Trim off any extra fabric on top and bottom to line each layer up

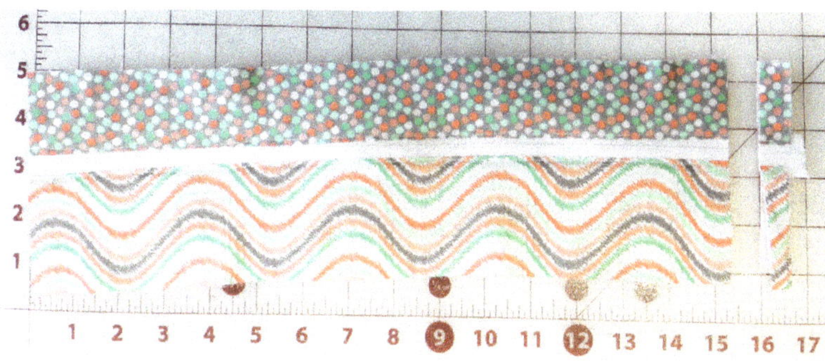

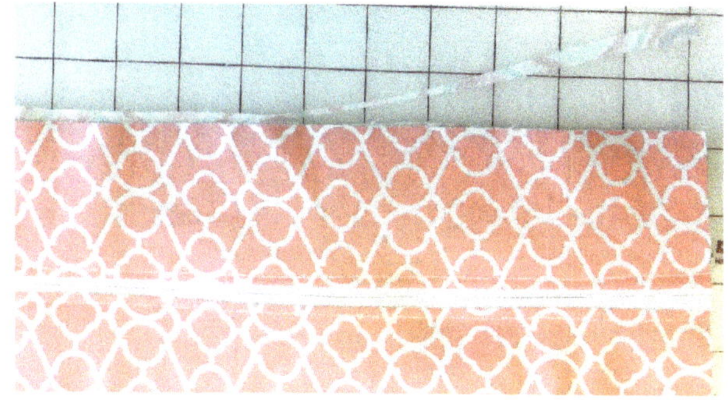

Step 8

-If your zipper already has a slider skip this step.

-Add your zipper slider at this point

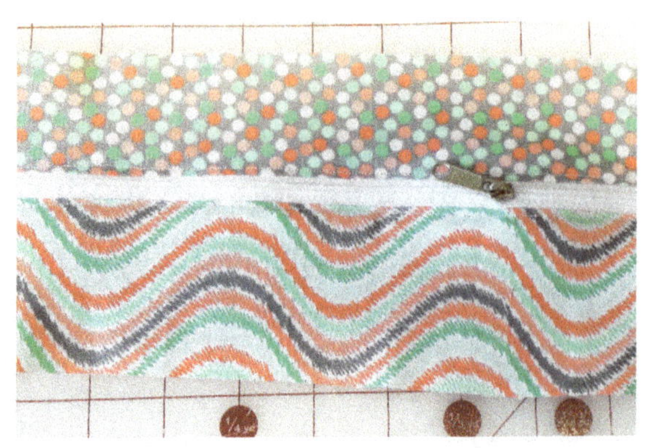

Step 9

-Baste a scant seam around the perimeter of the entire zipper panel through all layers.

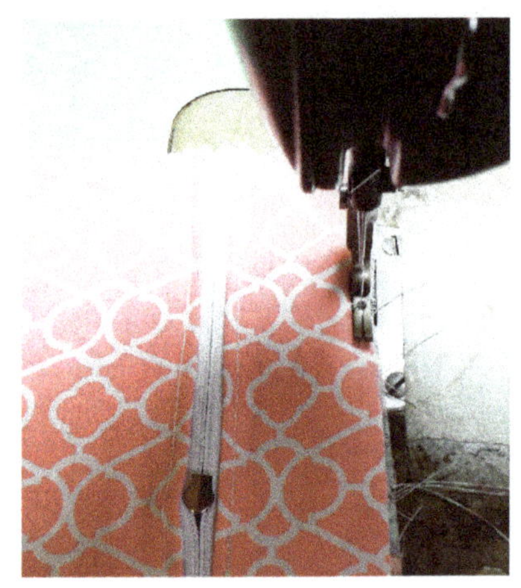

Step 10

-Attach back piece #1

- Place the outer fabric of piece #1 and lining fabric right sides together with the zipper panel in between making sure the zipper teeth are facing up towards the outer fabric of piece #1.

-Make sure the long edge of piece #1 is aligned with the short edge of the zipper panel. You will have excess fabric on the top and bottom, which will be trimmed off later.

-Pin in place.

-Outer fabric of piece #1 has fusible fleece attached.

-Sew through all layers along the edge of the fusible fleece.

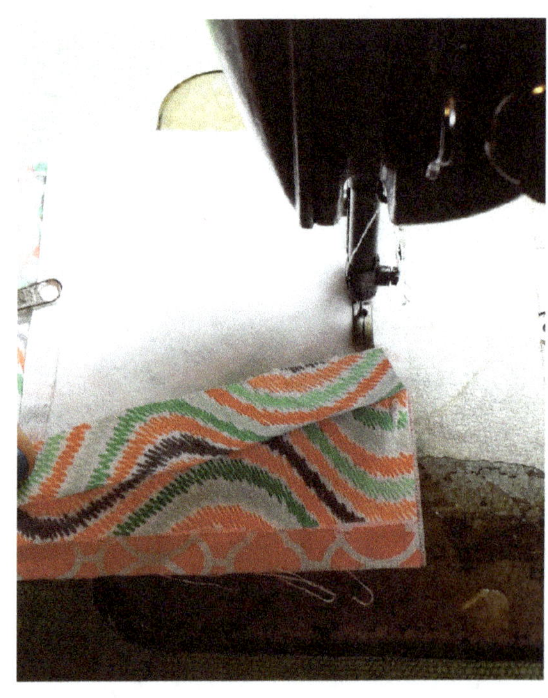

Step 11

-Flip both fabrics so wrong sides are together and top stitch along the seam near the edge.

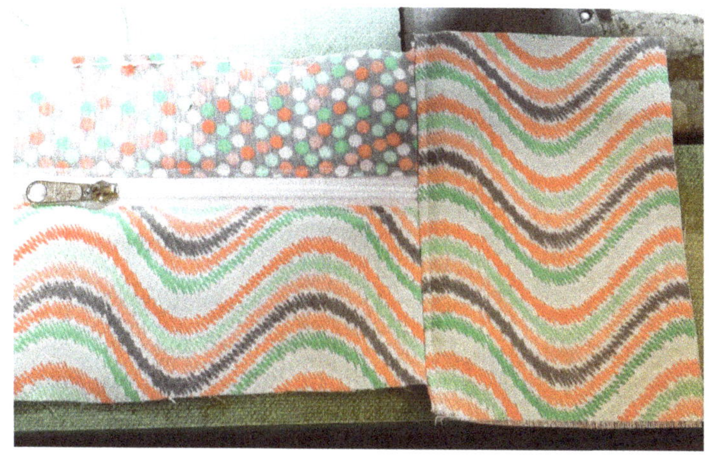

Step 12

-Fold seam allowance of the other side of piece #1 and press with iron.

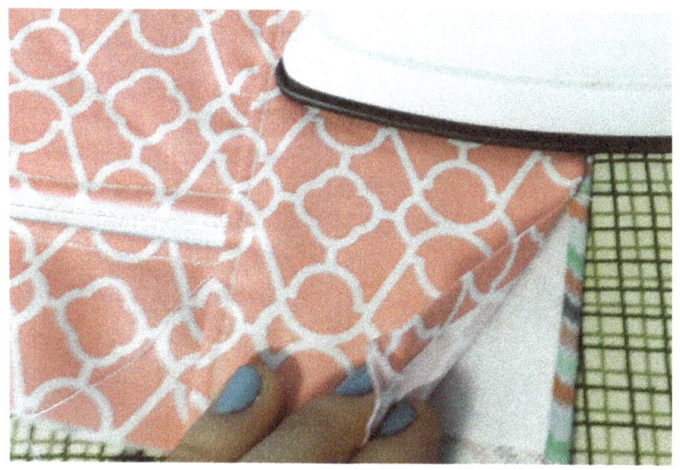

Step 13

-Insert the loose end of the zipper panel into the pressed edge you just created.

-Make sure to only insert about 1/4" / 6mm of your zipper panel.

-Pin through all layers and double check the zipper panel is is lined up at the top and bottom.

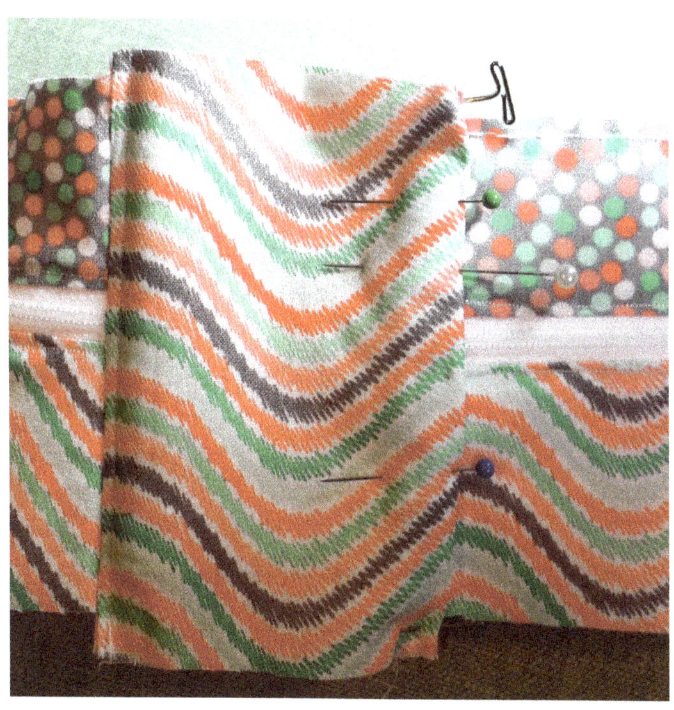

Step 14

-Sew through all layers.

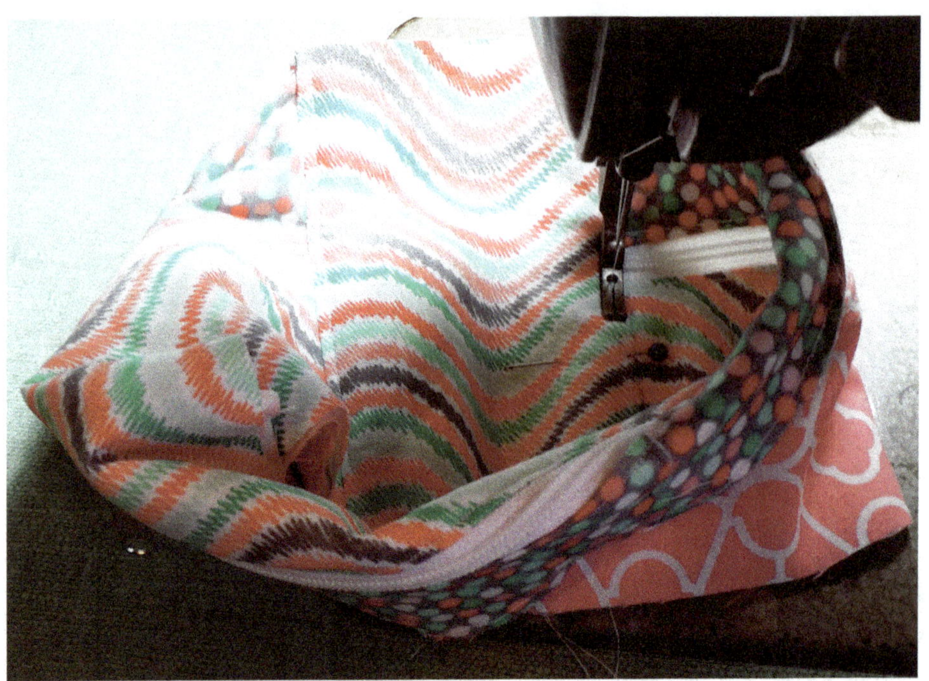

-It will look like this.

-Press with iron one more time.

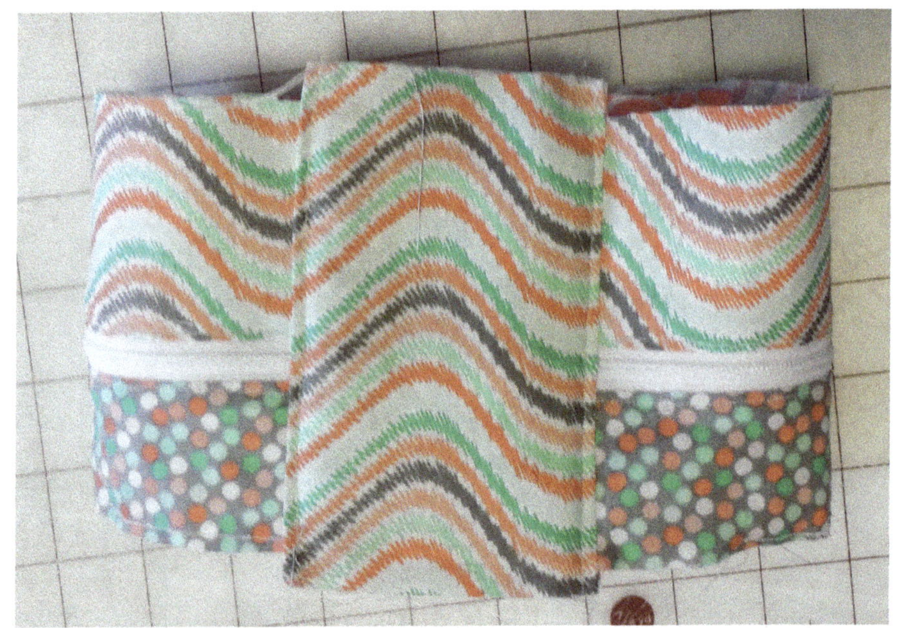

Step 15

-Trim off excess top and bottom of piece #1 to aslign it with the zipper panel.

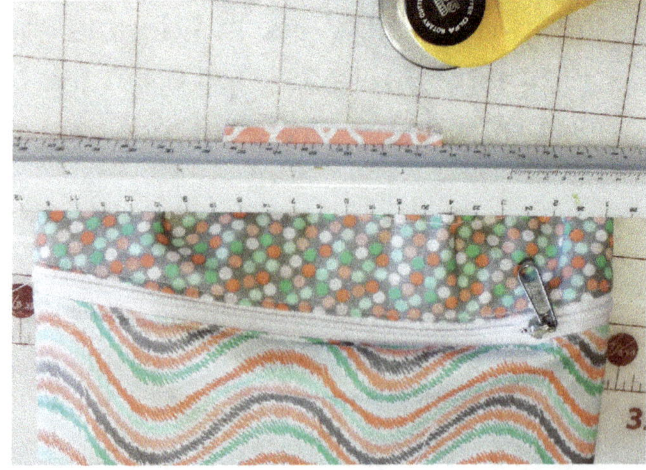

Step 16

-Place the outer fabric of piece #9 and lining fabric wrong sides together and baste a scant seam along the perimeter.

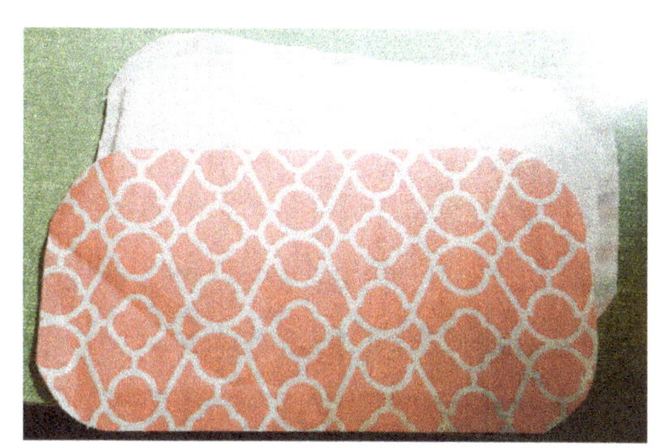

Step 17

-Align the raw edge of the piping with the raw edge of the outer fabric of the top piece #9 .

-Start at the middle of the long side. At the starting point turn the piping so you sew threw the cord.

-Overlap the piping at the end and sew through the cord.

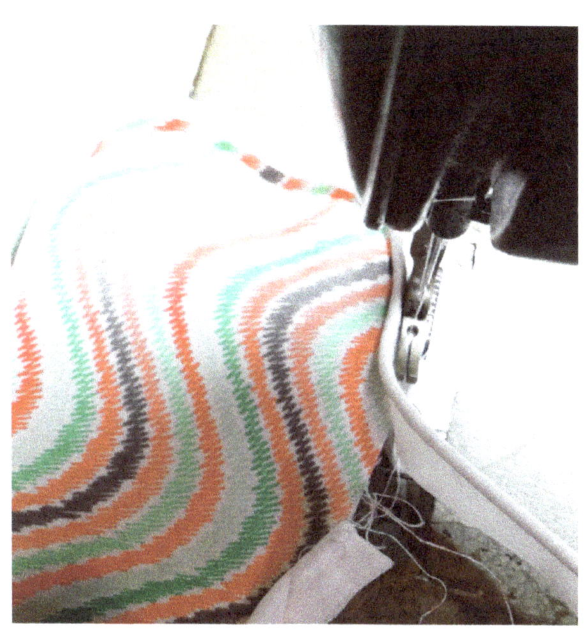

-Trim off excess and it will look like this.

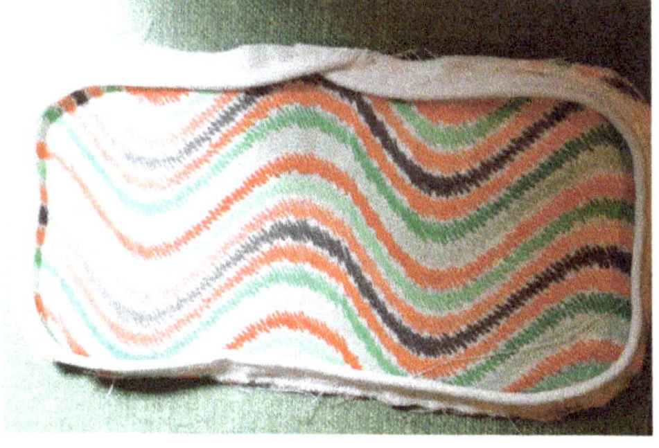

Step 18

- Make the handle.

-Place the both fabric pieces #8 right sides together and sew along the perimeter of the fusible fleece leaving one long edge open.

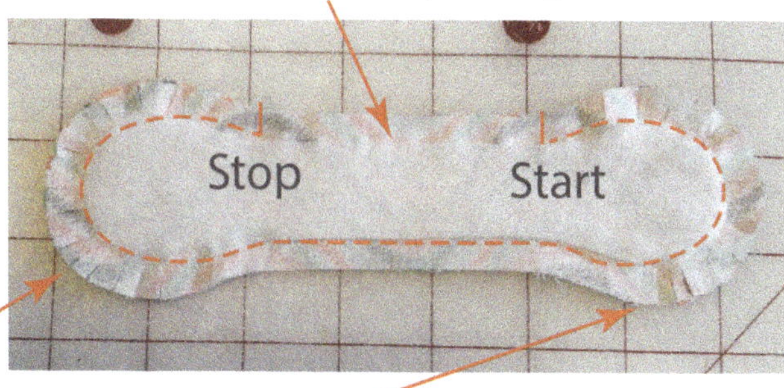

-Trim slits or notches around the round edges just up to the seam but don't cut through the seam.

Step 19

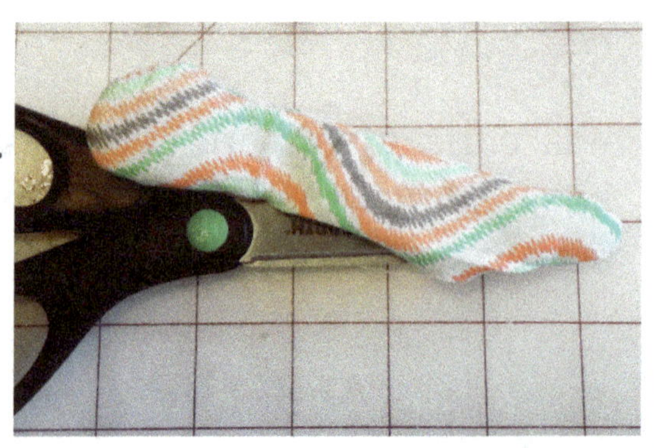

-Turn the handle right side out through the opening.

-Using rounded scissors or another dull point helps to push out the seam.

-Turn in the seam allowance of the opening and press with iron.

-Top stich around the perimeter of the handle

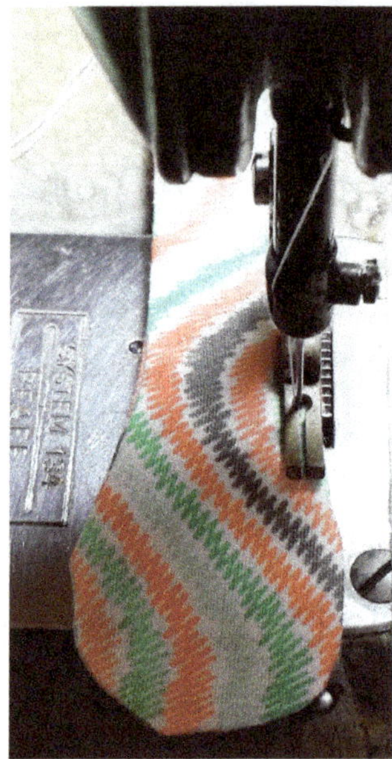

Step 20

-Attach the handle.

-Position the handle on the outer fabric top of our case, piece #9

-Stich through all layers

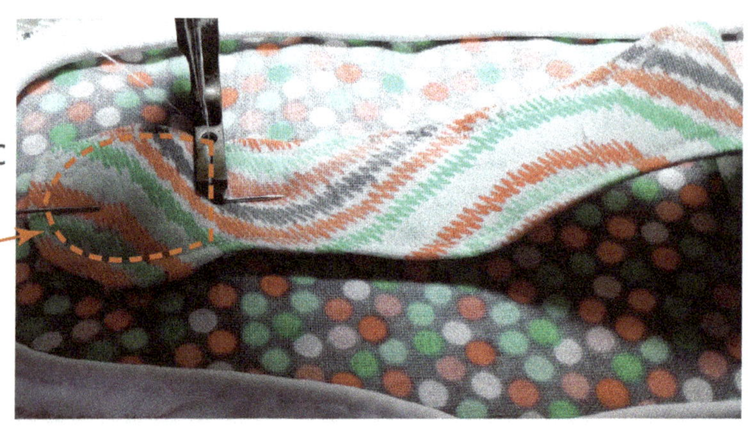

-It will look like this

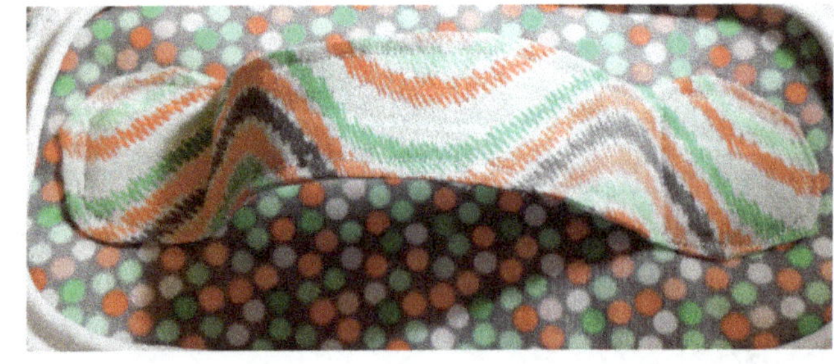

Step 21

-Mark the center points of the zipper panel.

-Fold the back piece #1 in half to find the center point and mark it with a pin..

-Hold the pinned side and fold in half again and mark the opposite point with a pin.

-Do the same for the other side until you have 4 points marked with pins that are equally spaced apart

-Do the same for your top and bottom pieces #9.

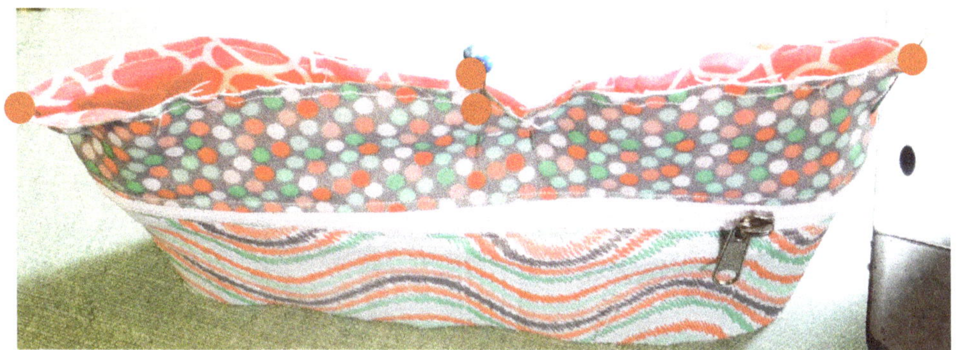

Step 22

-Working from the top of the zipper panel match the center point of the back piece #1 to the center point of the top piece where you started and ended the piping. (You want this start/stop point of the piping to be at the back of the case).

-Continue to match up the centerpoints and pin right sides together.

-Sew through all layers around the perimeter of the top piece making sure you don't catch the piping cord in the seam.

-Do the same for the bottom piece #1 on the other side of the zipper panel.

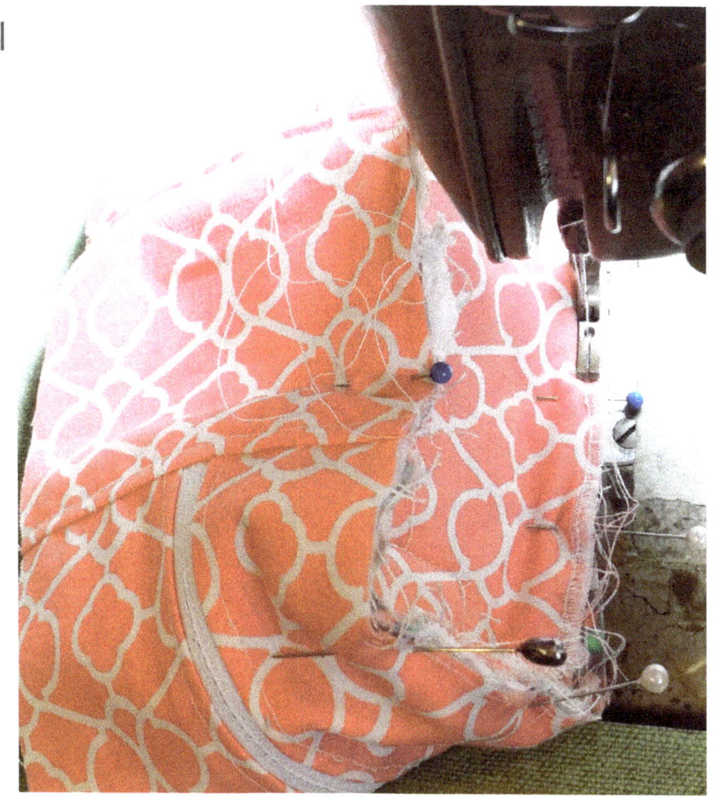

-Flip the case right side out and it will look like this.

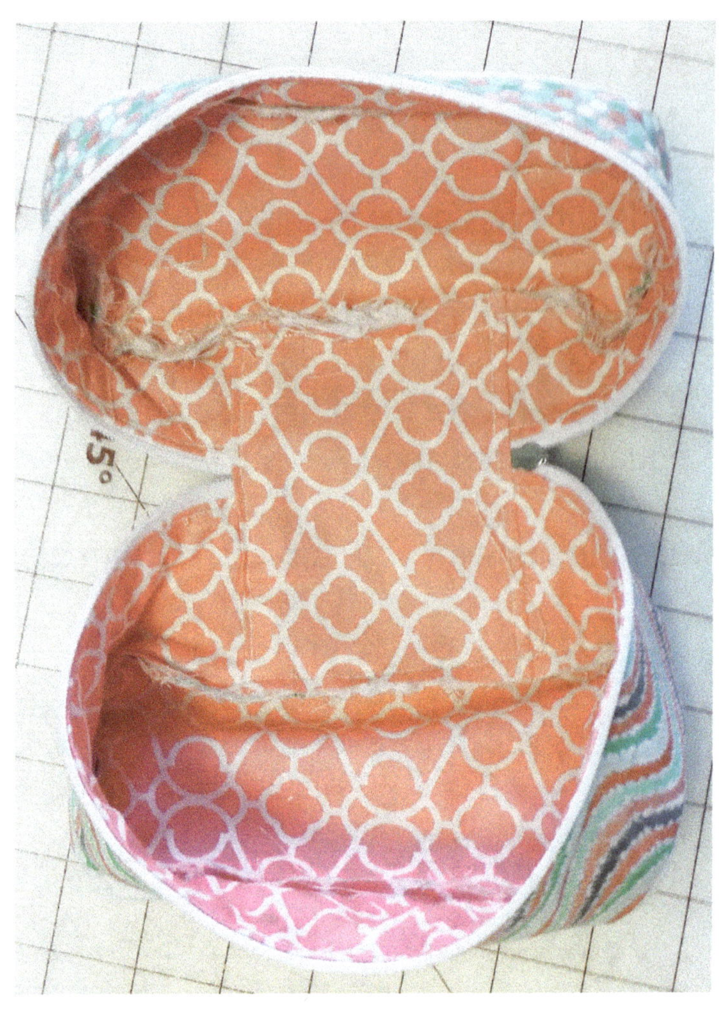

Step 23

-Make the interior.

-Fold the edges of piece #11 inward and stitch around the perimeter

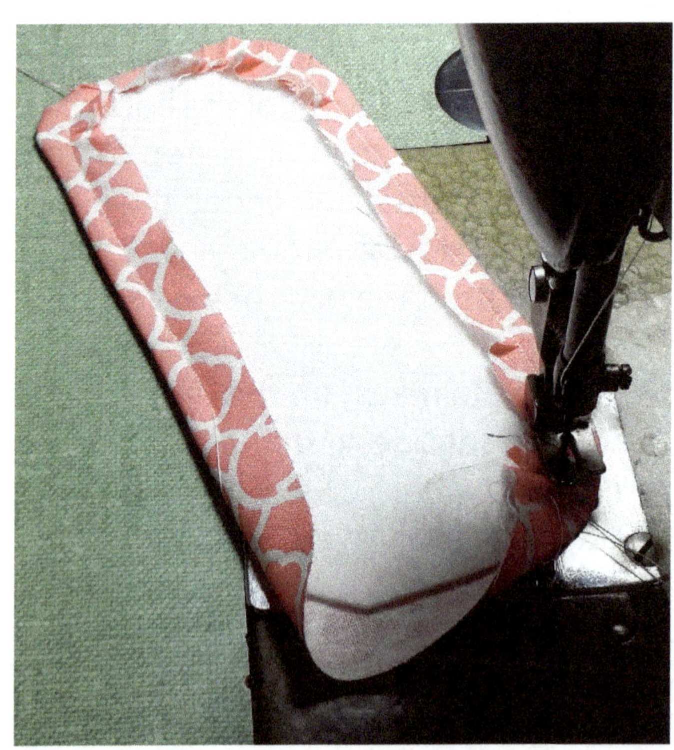

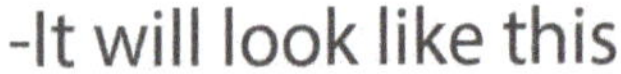

-It will look like this

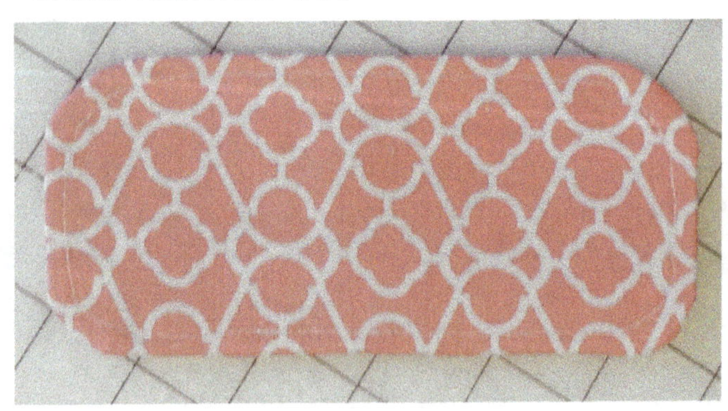

Step 23

-Turn the case wrong side out and hand sew the interior top and bottom piece #11 to the top and bottom of the case.

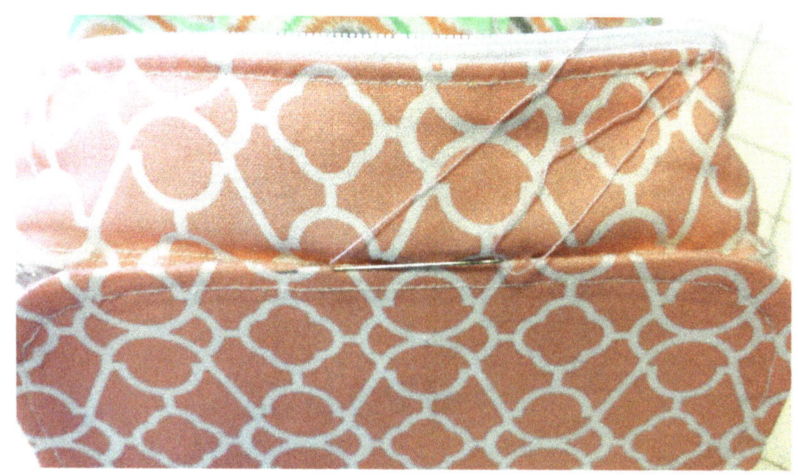

-Flip the case right side out and it will look like this.

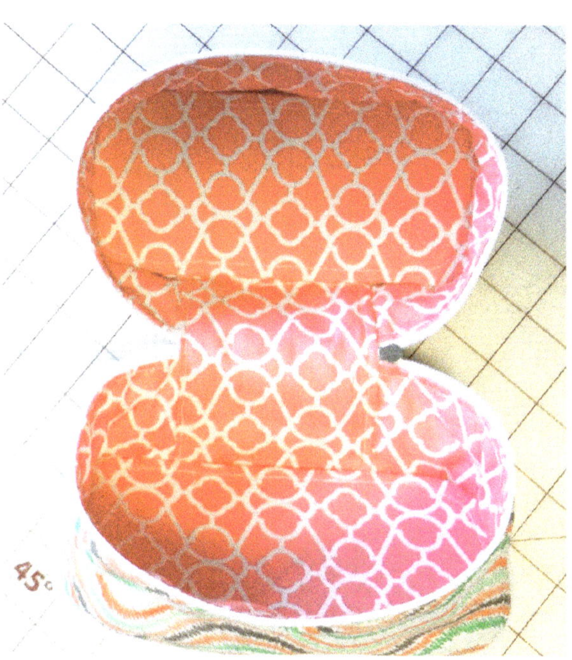

DONE!

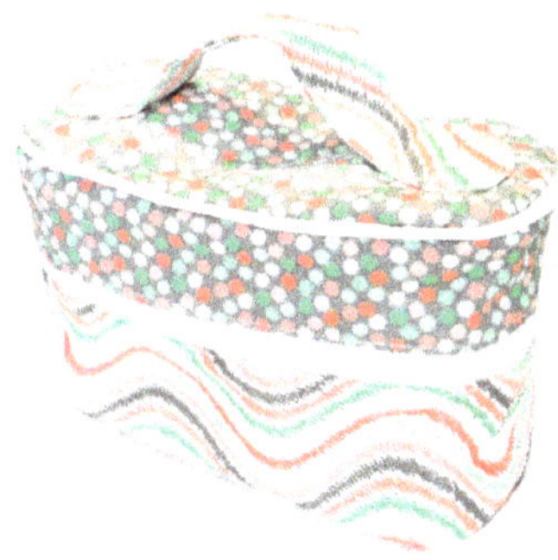

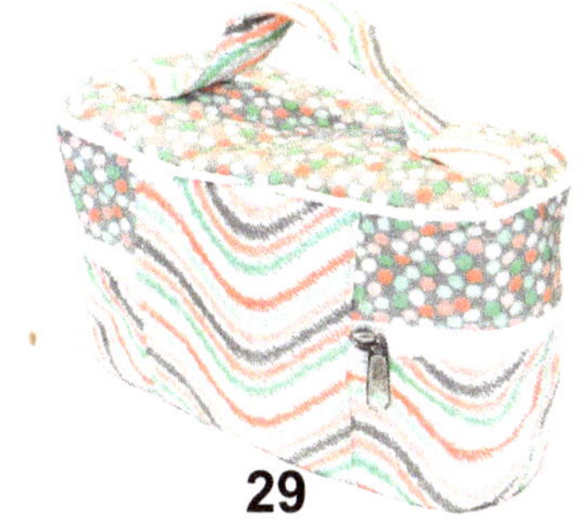

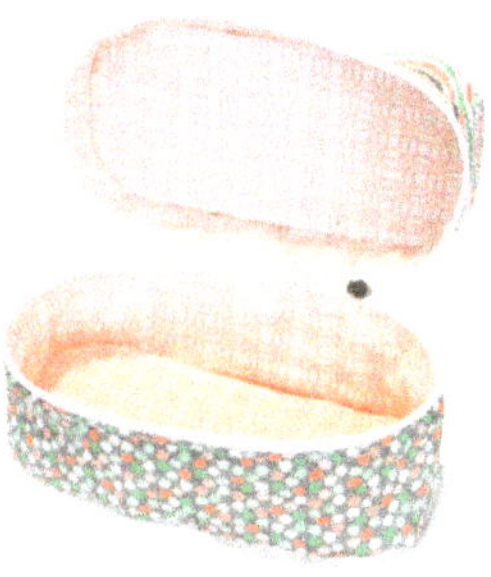

Coupon Organizer Pattern

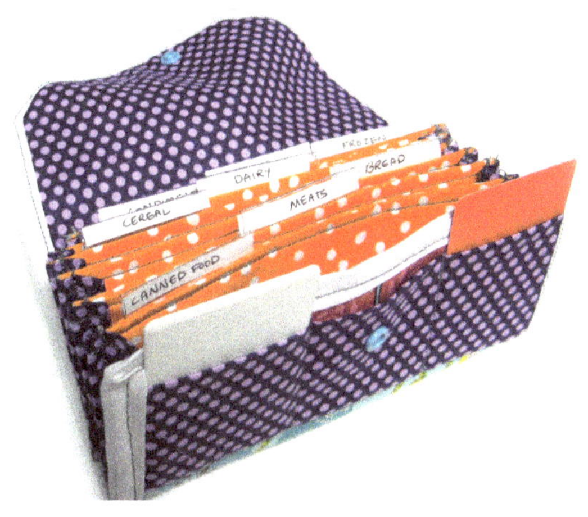

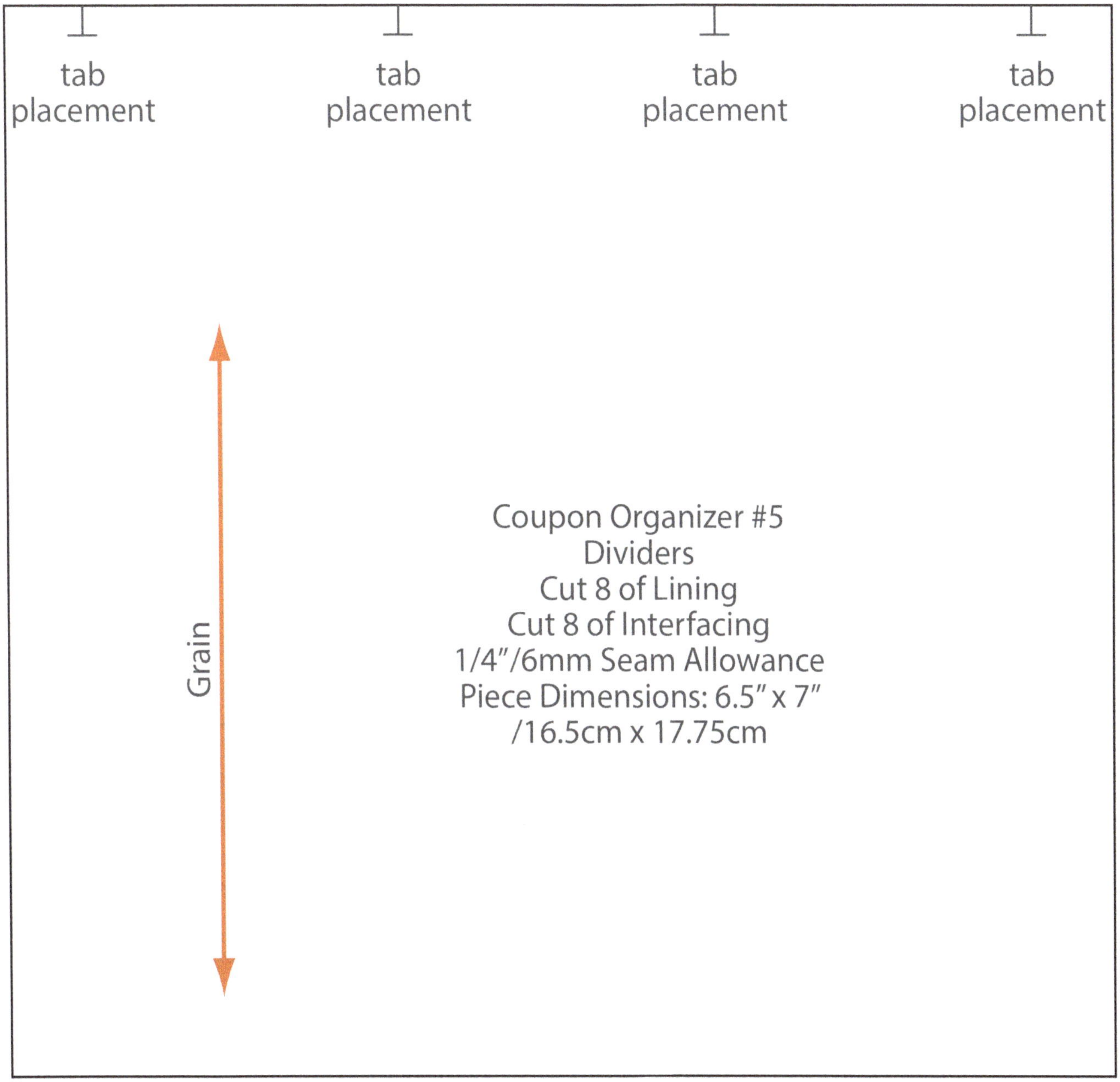

tab placement

tab placement

tab placement

tab placement

Grain

Coupon Organizer #5
Dividers
Cut 8 of Lining
Cut 8 of Interfacing
1/4"/6mm Seam Allowance
Piece Dimensions: 6.5" x 7"
/16.5cm x 17.75cm

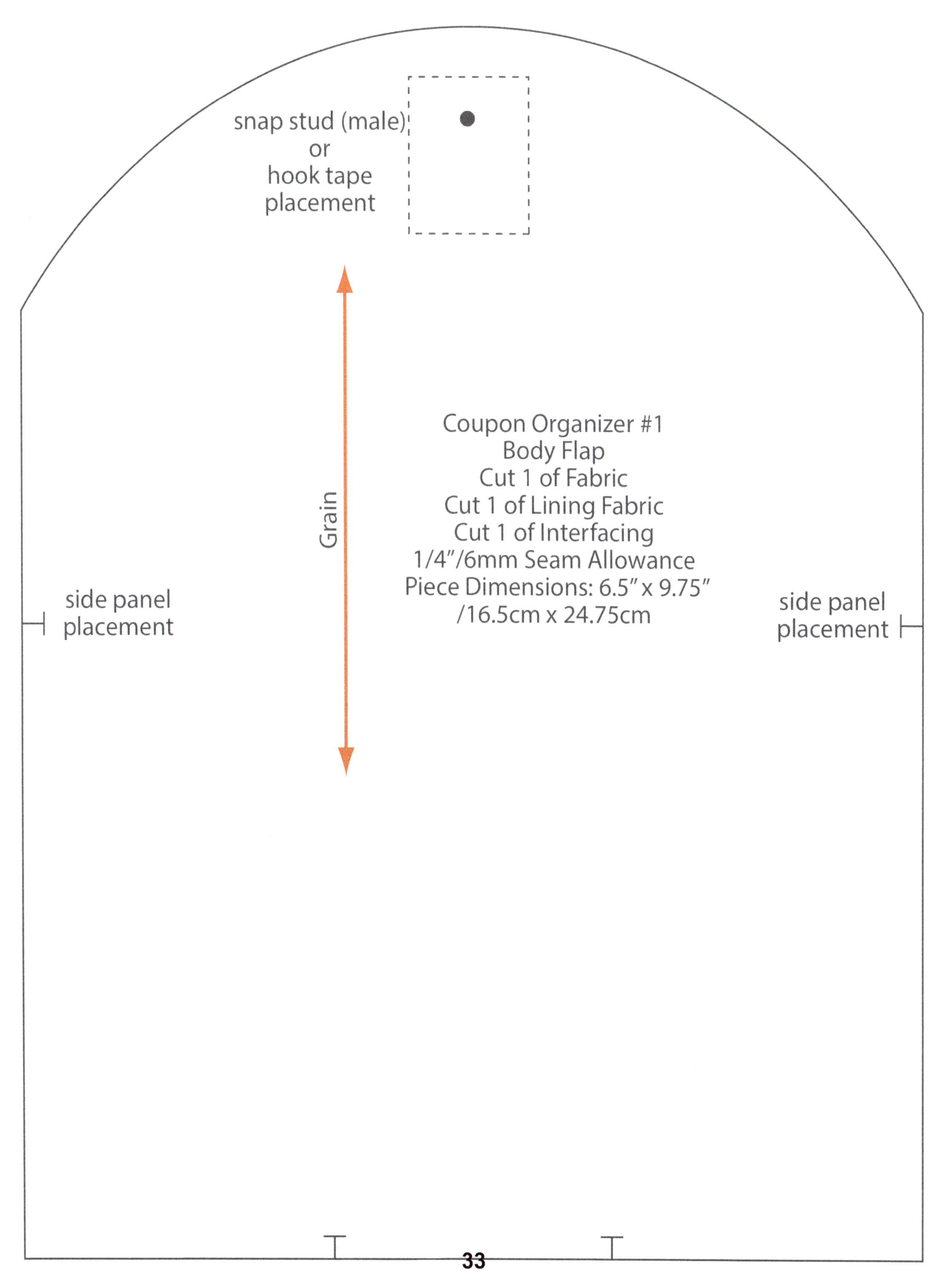
snap stud (male)
or
hook tape
placement
Grain
Coupon Organizer #1
Body Flap
Cut 1 of Fabric
Cut 1 of Lining Fabric
Cut 1 of Interfacing
1/4"/6mm Seam Allowance
Piece Dimensions: 6.5" x 9.75"
/16.5cm x 24.75cm
side panel
placement
side panel
placement

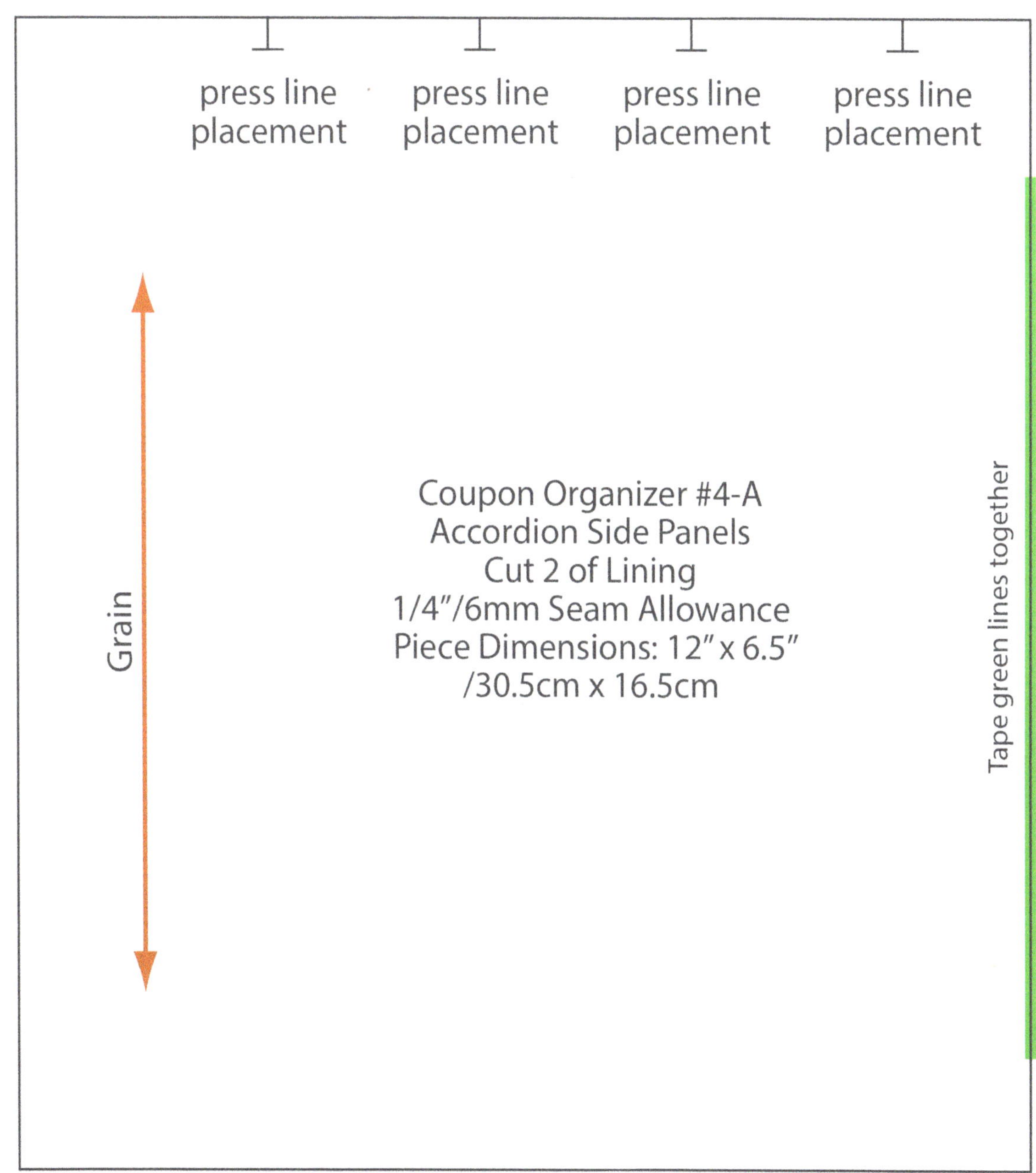
press line placement
press line placement
press line placement
press line placement
Coupon Organizer #4-A
Accordion Side Panels
Cut 2 of Lining
1/4"/6mm Seam Allowance
Piece Dimensions: 12" x 6.5"
/30.5cm x 16.5cm
Grain
Tape green lines together

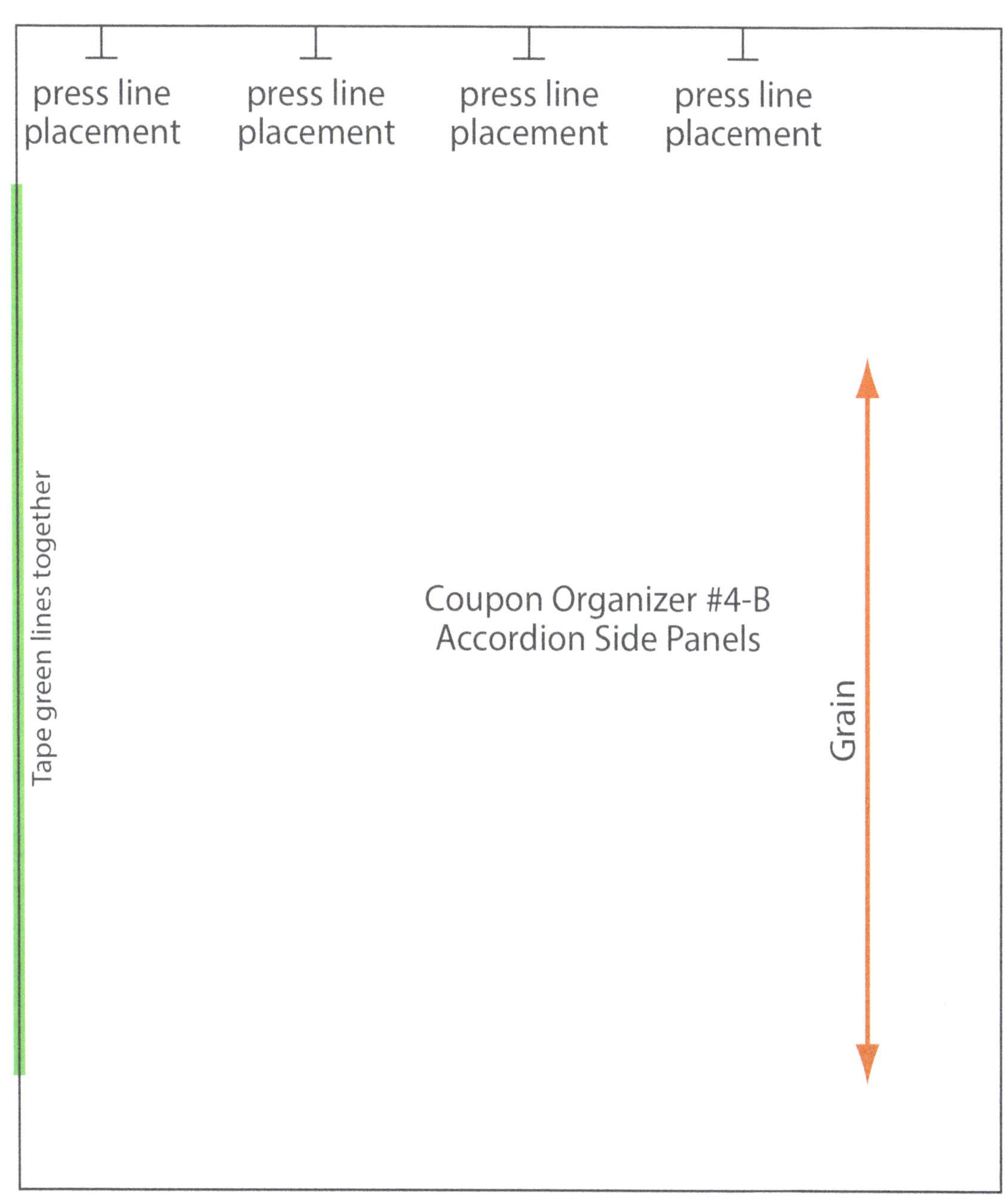

Coupon Organizer #6
Divider Tabs
Cut 8 of Clear Vinyl
1/4"/6mm Seam Allowance
Piece Dimensions: 2" x 1.25"
/5cm x 3cm

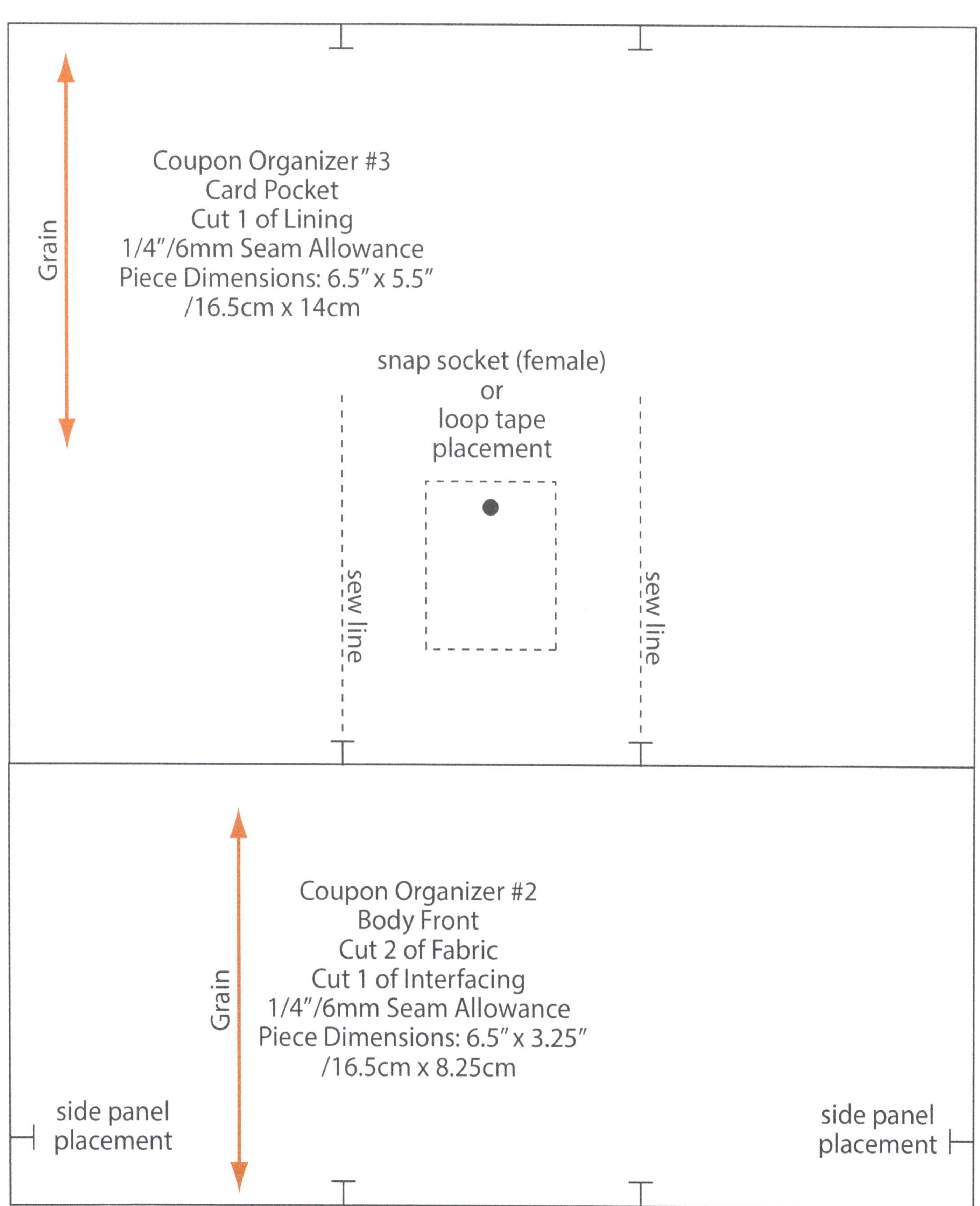
Coupon Organizer #3
Card Pocket
Cut 1 of Lining
1/4″/6mm Seam Allowance
Piece Dimensions: 6.5″ x 5.5″
/16.5cm x 14cm
Grain
snap socket (female)
or
loop tape
placement
sew line
sew line
Coupon Organizer #2
Body Front
Cut 2 of Fabric
Cut 1 of Interfacing
1/4″/6mm Seam Allowance
Piece Dimensions: 6.5″ x 3.25″
/16.5cm x 8.25cm
Grain
side panel
placement
side panel
placement

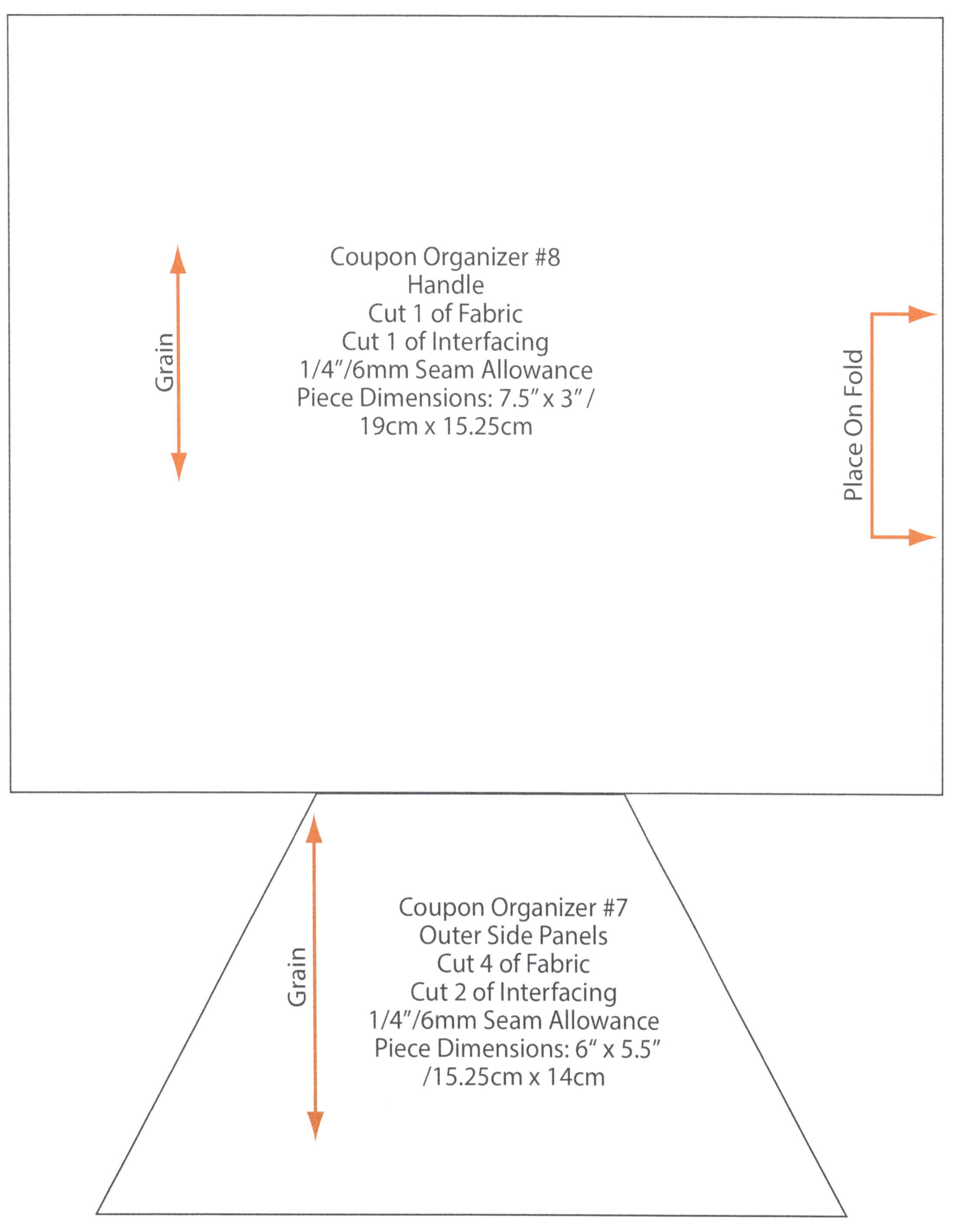
Coupon Organizer #8
Handle
Cut 1 of Fabric
Cut 1 of Interfacing
1/4"/6mm Seam Allowance
Piece Dimensions: 7.5" x 3" /
19cm x 15.25cm
Grain
Place On Fold
Coupon Organizer #7
Outer Side Panels
Cut 4 of Fabric
Cut 2 of Interfacing
1/4"/6mm Seam Allowance
Piece Dimensions: 6" x 5.5"
/15.25cm x 14cm
Grain

Coupon Organizer Tutorial

Materials:
-Base fabric - light weight
-Lining fabric - light weight
-Fusible Interfacing
-Vinyl or 1 sheet of printable fabric or 1 sheet of iron transfer paper
-1 Snap set or 1" x 1.5" / 25mm x 38mm hook and loop tape
-Binding tape

Step 1

-Cut out the patterns.
Be sure to select "do not scale" in your printer settings.

Step 2

-Position the pattern pieces on the fabric so the grain line runs parallel to the grain or selvage of the fabric. (If you have directional fabric as shown in photo with a clear top and bottom to the design place the grain line parallel to the design).

-Mark all notches, lines and dots on the fabric (do not mark notches on piece #4 until step 8)

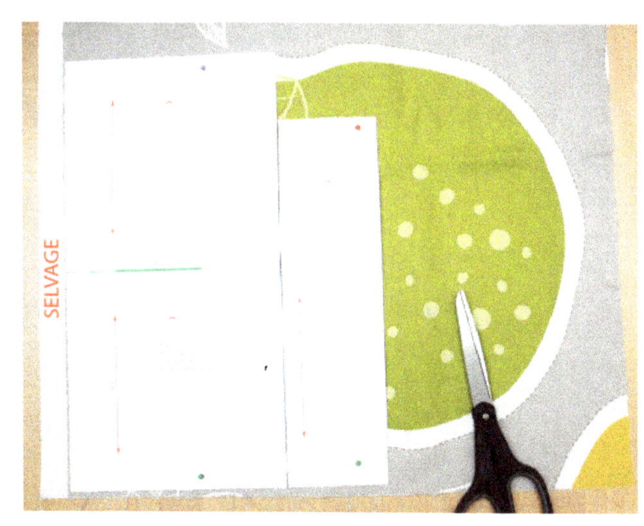

Step 3

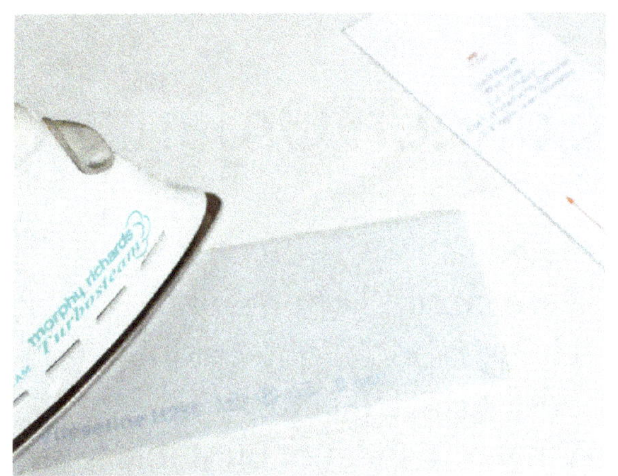

-Iron the interfacing onto the wrong side of base fabric of pieces #1, and #2, and lining fabric of all eight #5 pieces according to the manufacturer's instructions.

Step 4

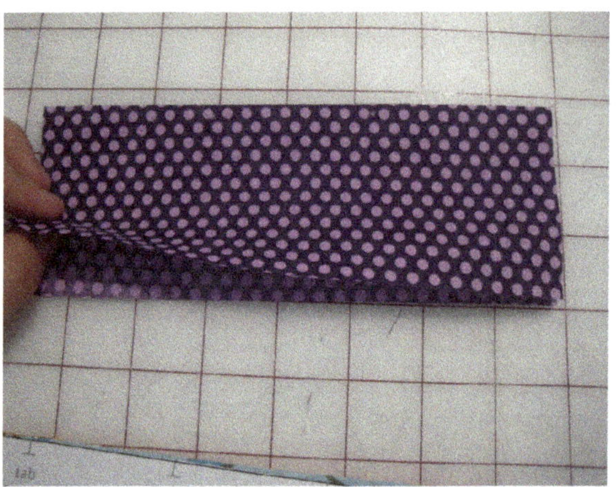

-Make the card pocket

-Fold piece #3 in half matching the notches and iron

-Add the snap socket with scrap piece of fabric in in betwen to reinforce the fabric
 or sew on the loop tape

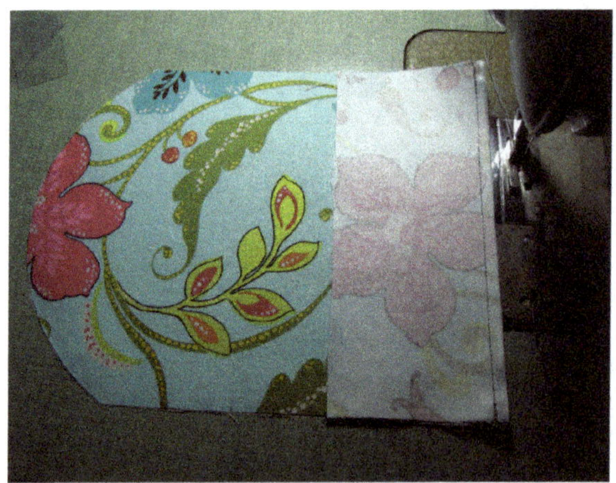

-Sandwich card pocket between piece #1 and #2 with right side facing towards piece #1 matching notches and stitch through all layers

**TIP - make sure the side of the pocket you want to see when you open your organizer is facing piece #1 especially if you are using directional fabric

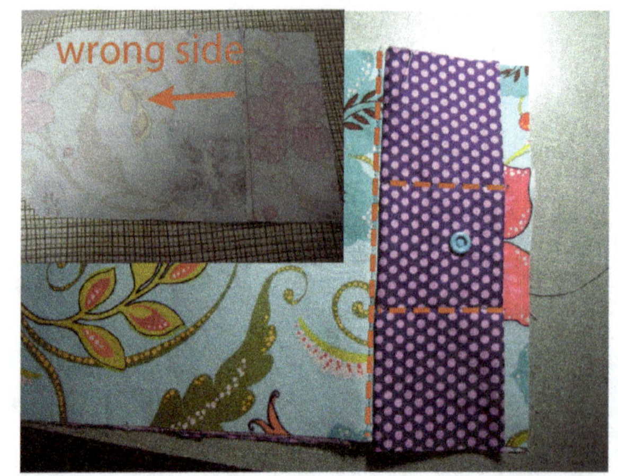

-Press seam towards top (curved end) and topstitch along seam

-Top stitch along sew lines of card pocket as indicated by the pattern to form 3 card pockets

Step 5

-Sew piece #1 and #2 of lining fabric right sides together matching notches

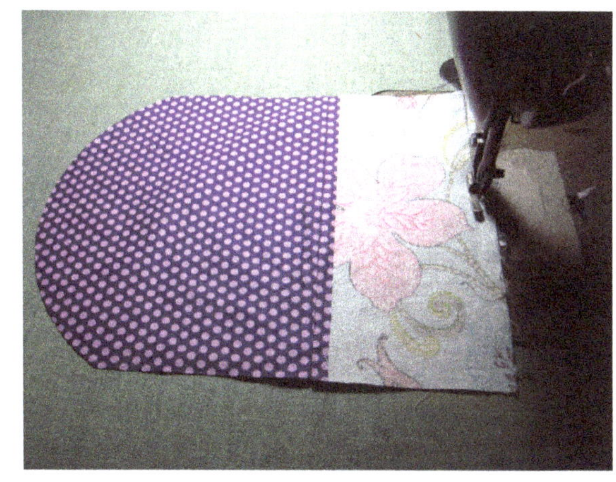

-Press seam towards bottom and topstitch along seam

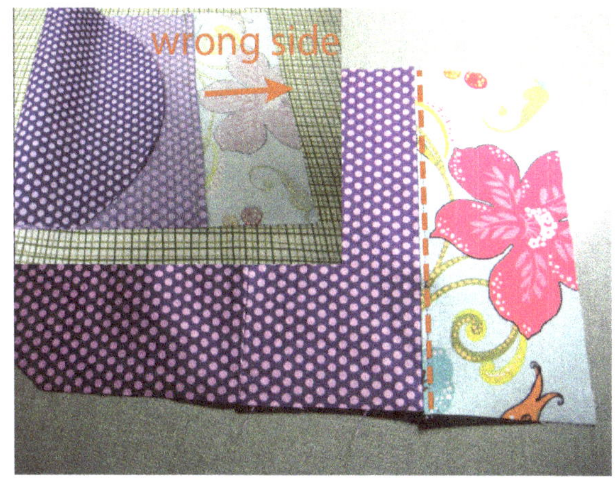

Step 6

-Make dividers

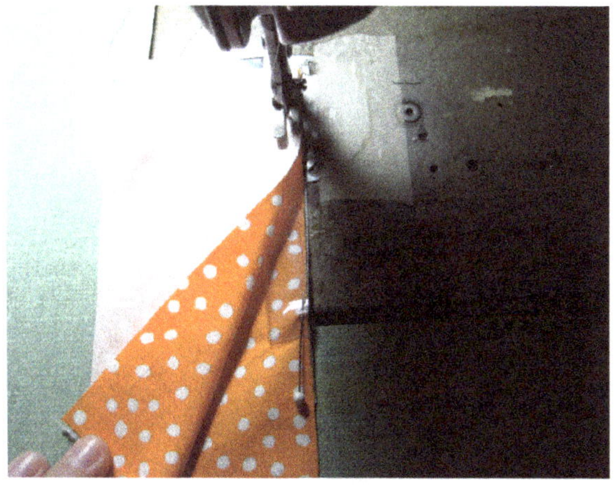

-Fold piece #5 in half perpendicular to the grain and towrds tab placement marks right sides together

-Sandwich a vinyl tab or fabric tab between the opening at second mark indicated by pattern and stitch

-Repeat for remaining 7 dividers being sure to place tabs at marks indicated by the pattern as follows:
3 tabs at first mark
2 tabs at second mark
2 tabs at third mark

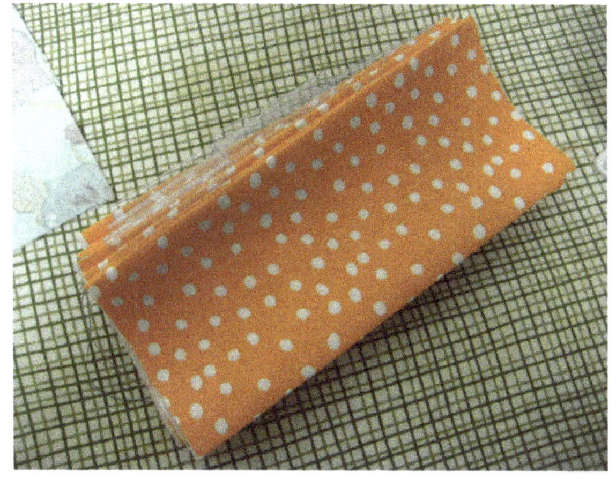

-Turn fabric right side out and press careful not to melt the vinyl

-Topstitch over seam

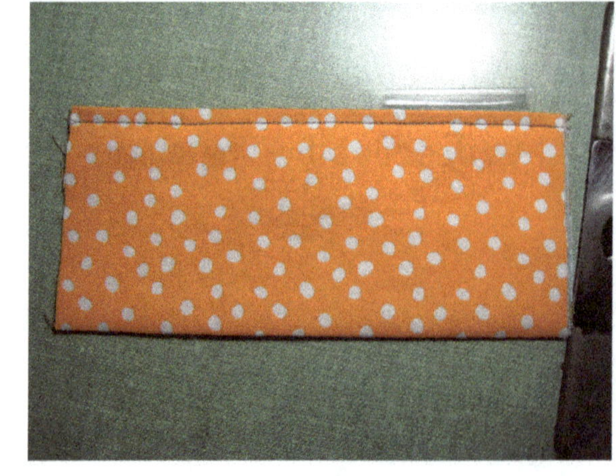

Step 7

-Make the accordion side panels

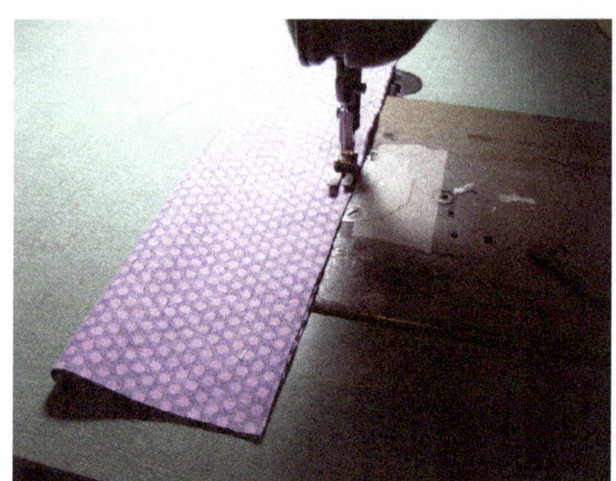

-Fold piece #4 in half perpendicular to the grain right sides together and stitch the long edge

-Position seam towards the middle and press open

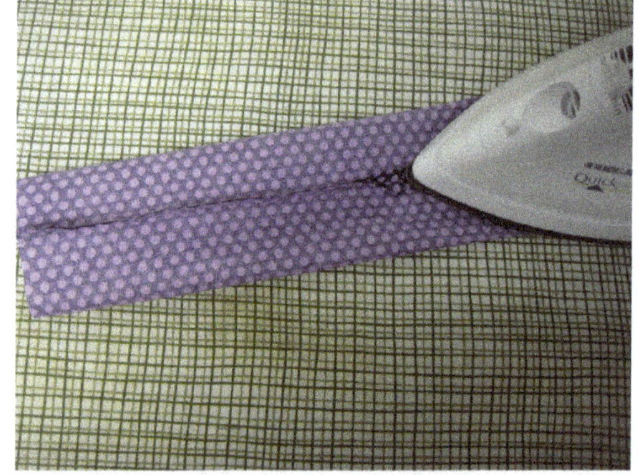

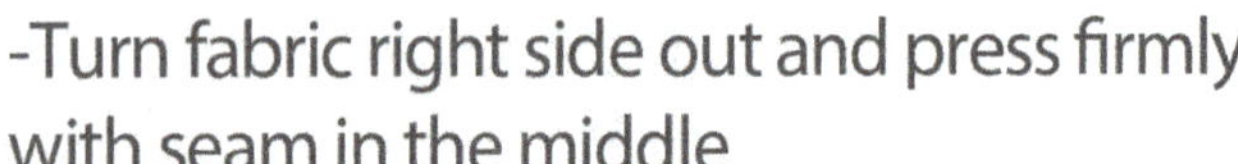

-Turn fabric right side out and press firmly with seam in the middle

-Top stitch close to both long edges

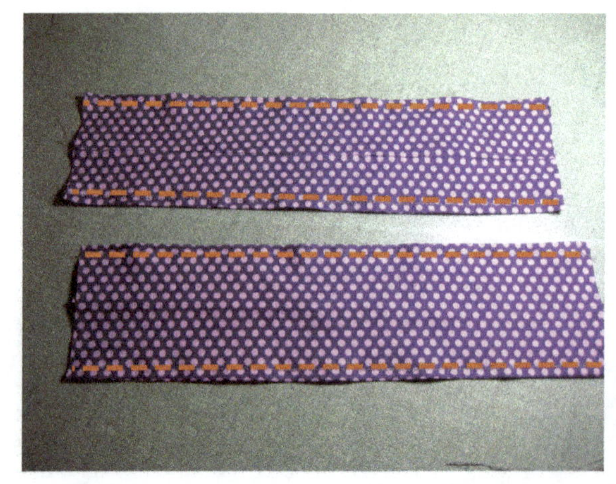

Step 8

-Create the folds

-Mark press lines from pattern piece

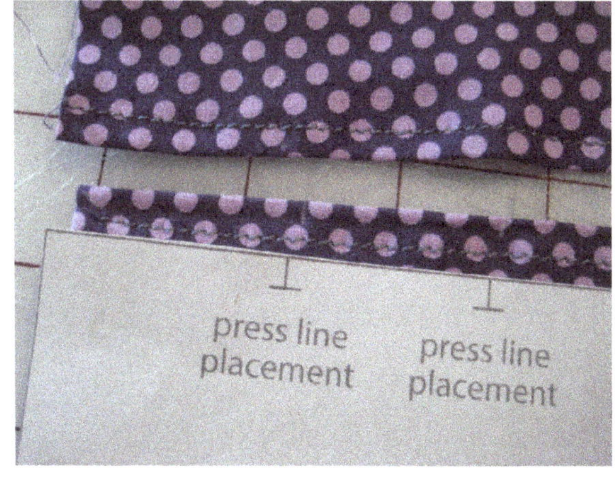

-Fold each line with middle seam facing in and iron firmly along press lines to form 8 folds

-(Optional) fold up the accordion and pin or clip in place to set the folds then set aside. Take a break and have a cup of tea!

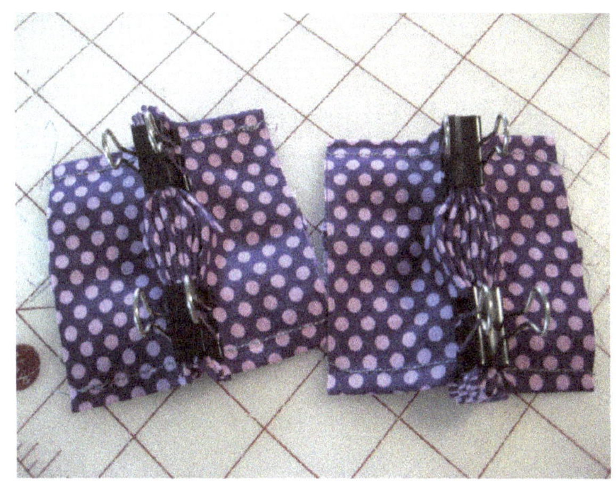

Step 9

-Assemble the dividers

-Insert divider inside pressed fold of accordion side panel and sew

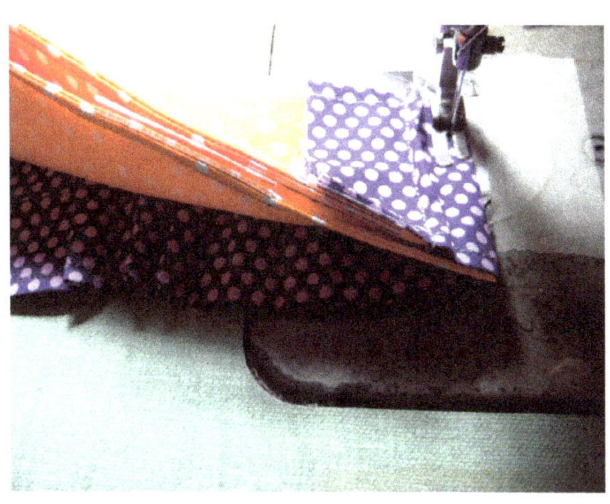

-Continue with remaining dividers being sure that all tabs are in the correct order and facing the same direction

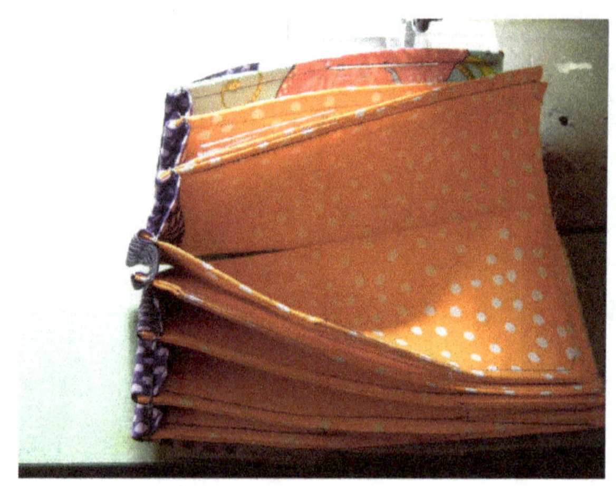

-Repeat with other side panel

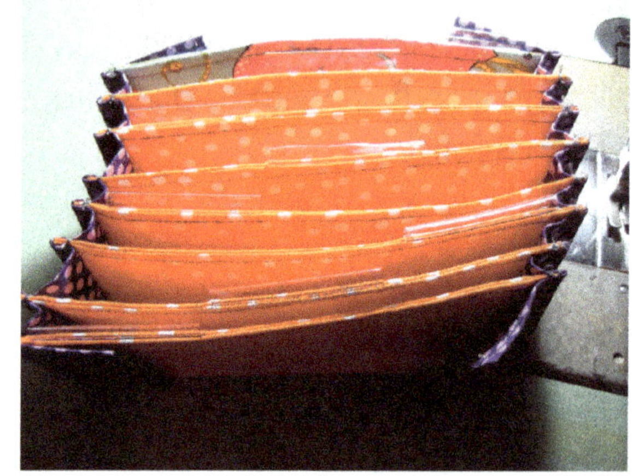

Step 10

-Assemble the organizer

-Line up the body lining and body outside wrong sides together

-Add the snap or hook tape as indicated by the pattern through all layers

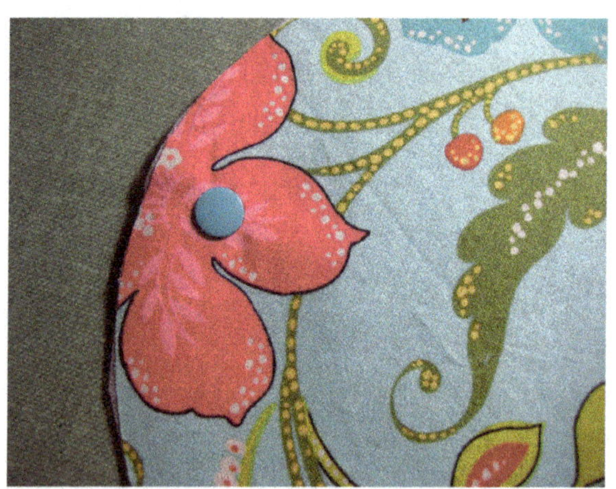

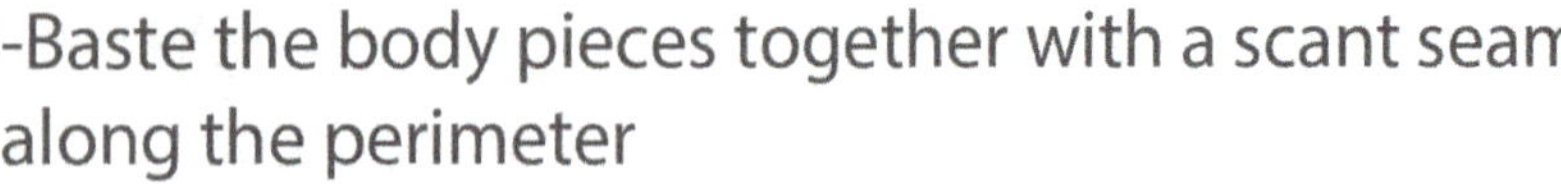

-Baste the body pieces together with a scant seam along the perimeter

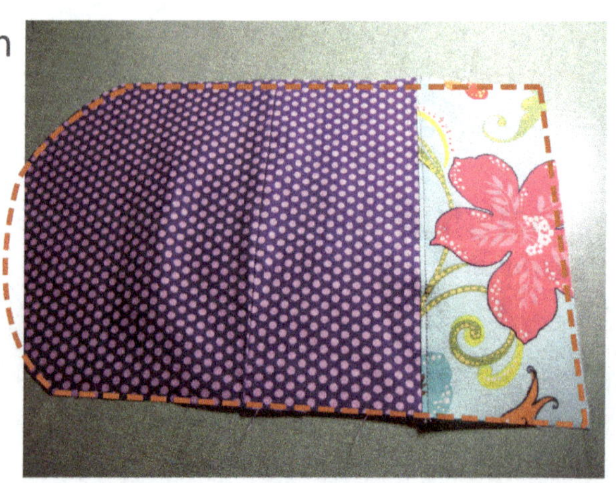

-Pin the accordion ends to the body at marks indicated by the pattern.

- Baste a scant seam

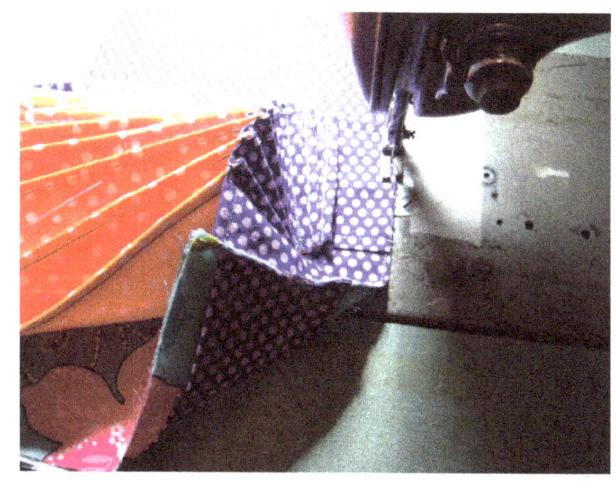

-Sew binding around perimeter of organizer starting at the side

-Fold corners at a 45 degree angle to create a flat seam

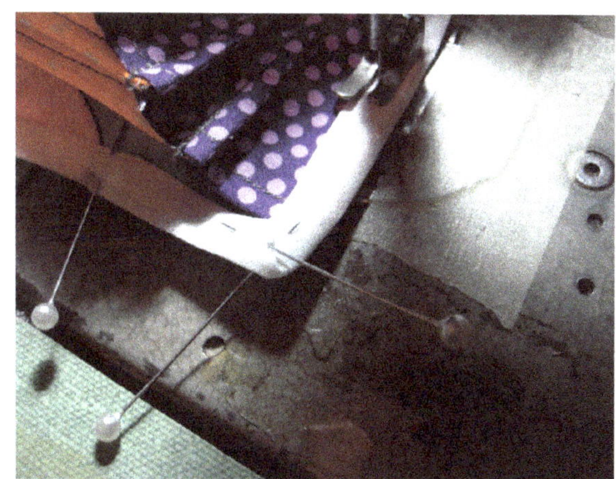

-Tuck in the end of the binding by folding under and stitching

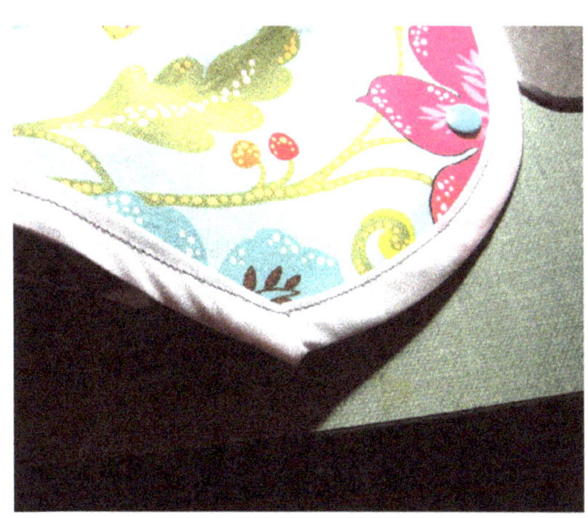

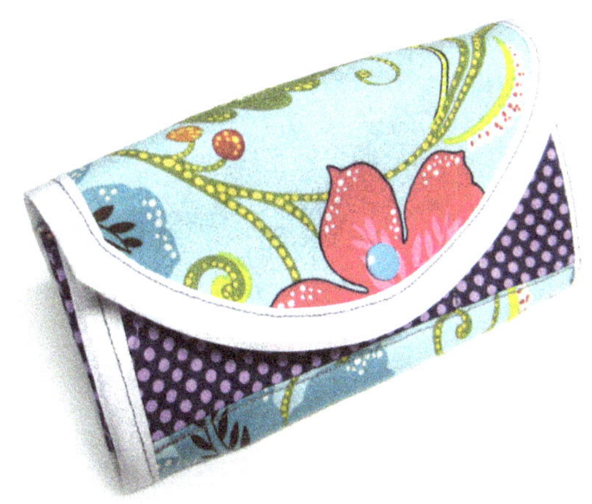

Lady Pad Patterns

Materials:
- Absorbent fabric (fleece, sherpa)
- Waterproof fabric (PUL)
- Soaking Fabric (fleece, flannel)
- Snaps or hook & loop

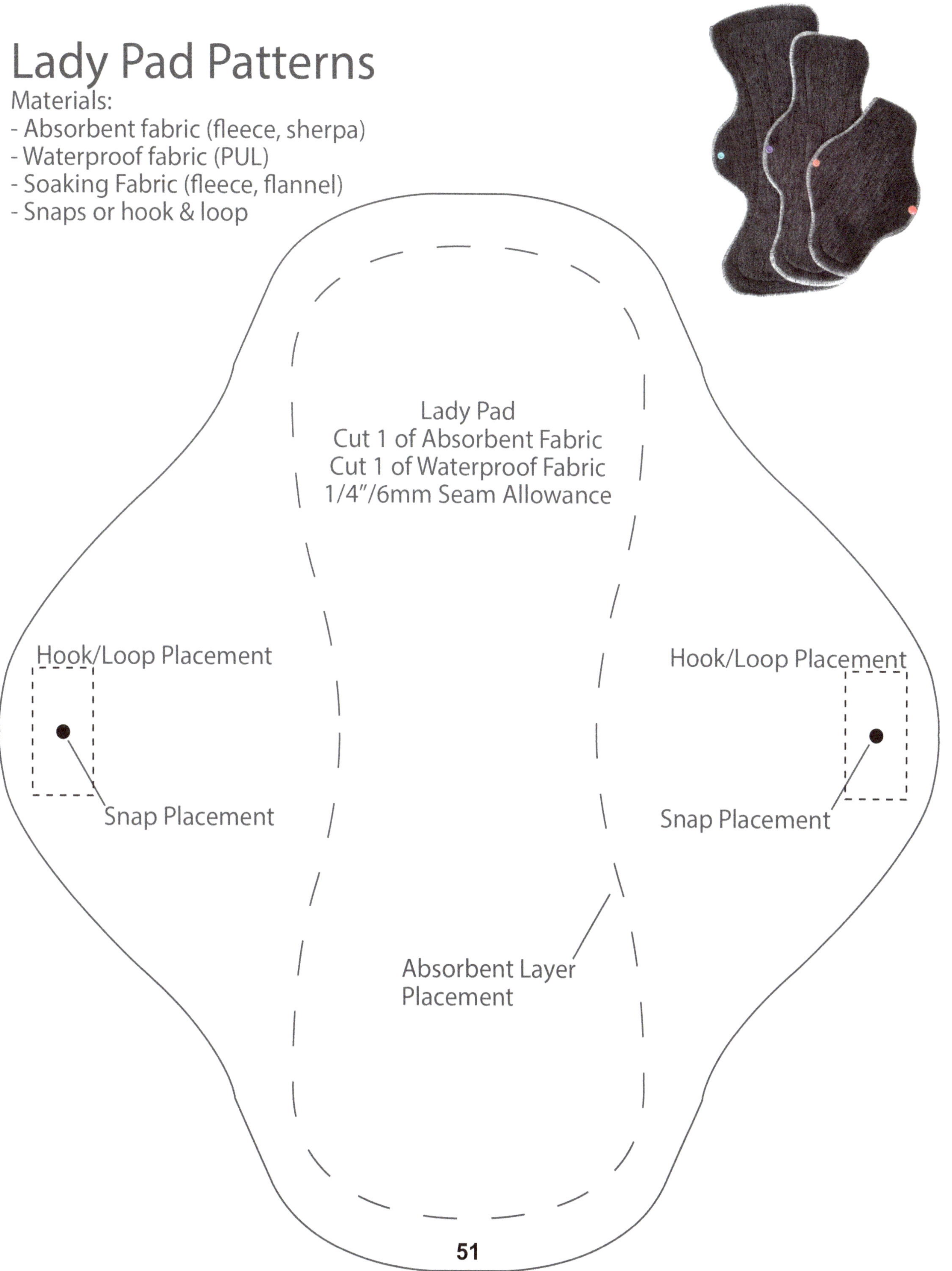

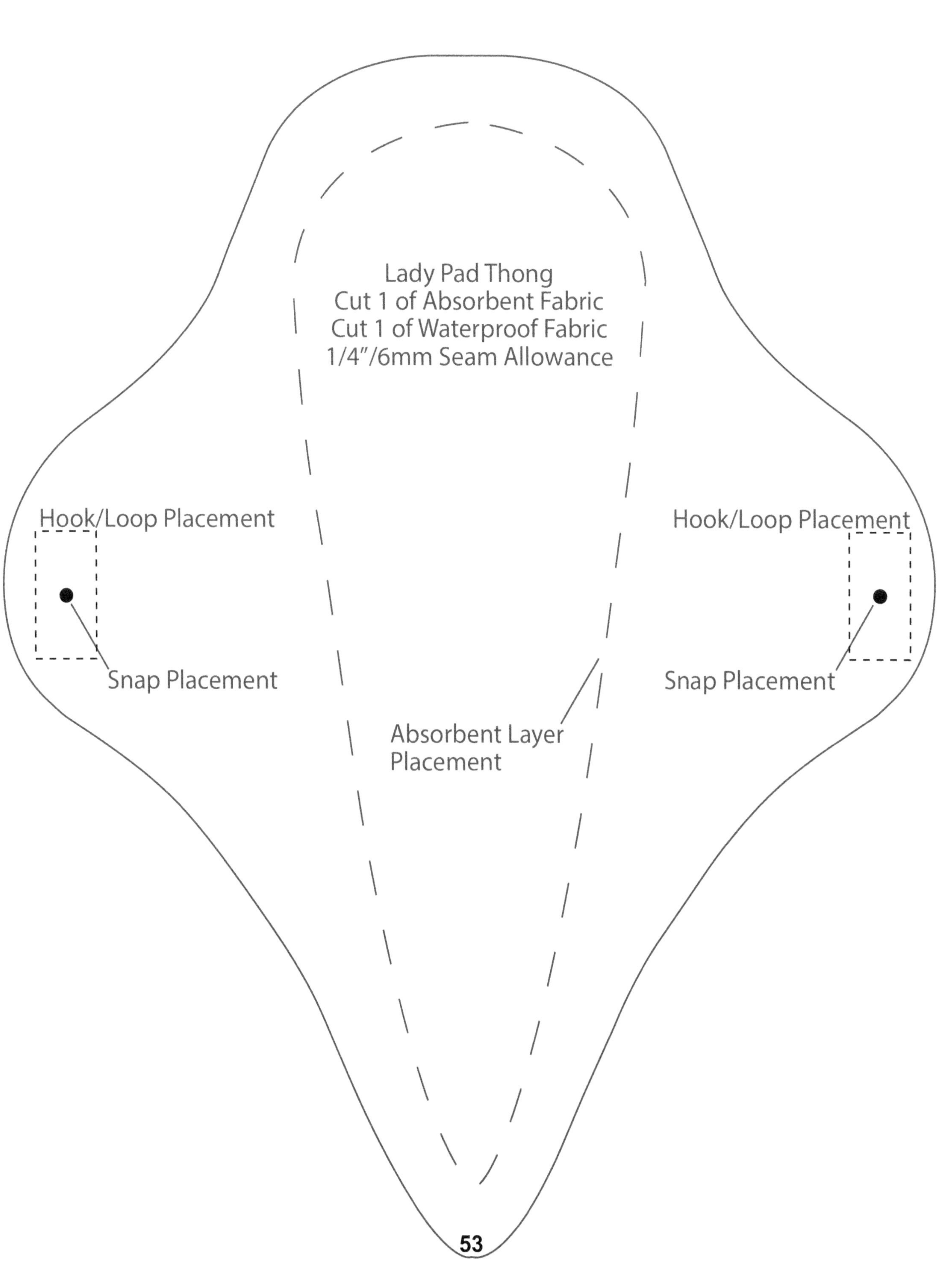
Lady Pad Thong
Cut 1 of Absorbent Fabric
Cut 1 of Waterproof Fabric
1/4"/6mm Seam Allowance
Hook/Loop Placement
Hook/Loop Placement
Snap Placement
Snap Placement
Absorbent Layer
Placement

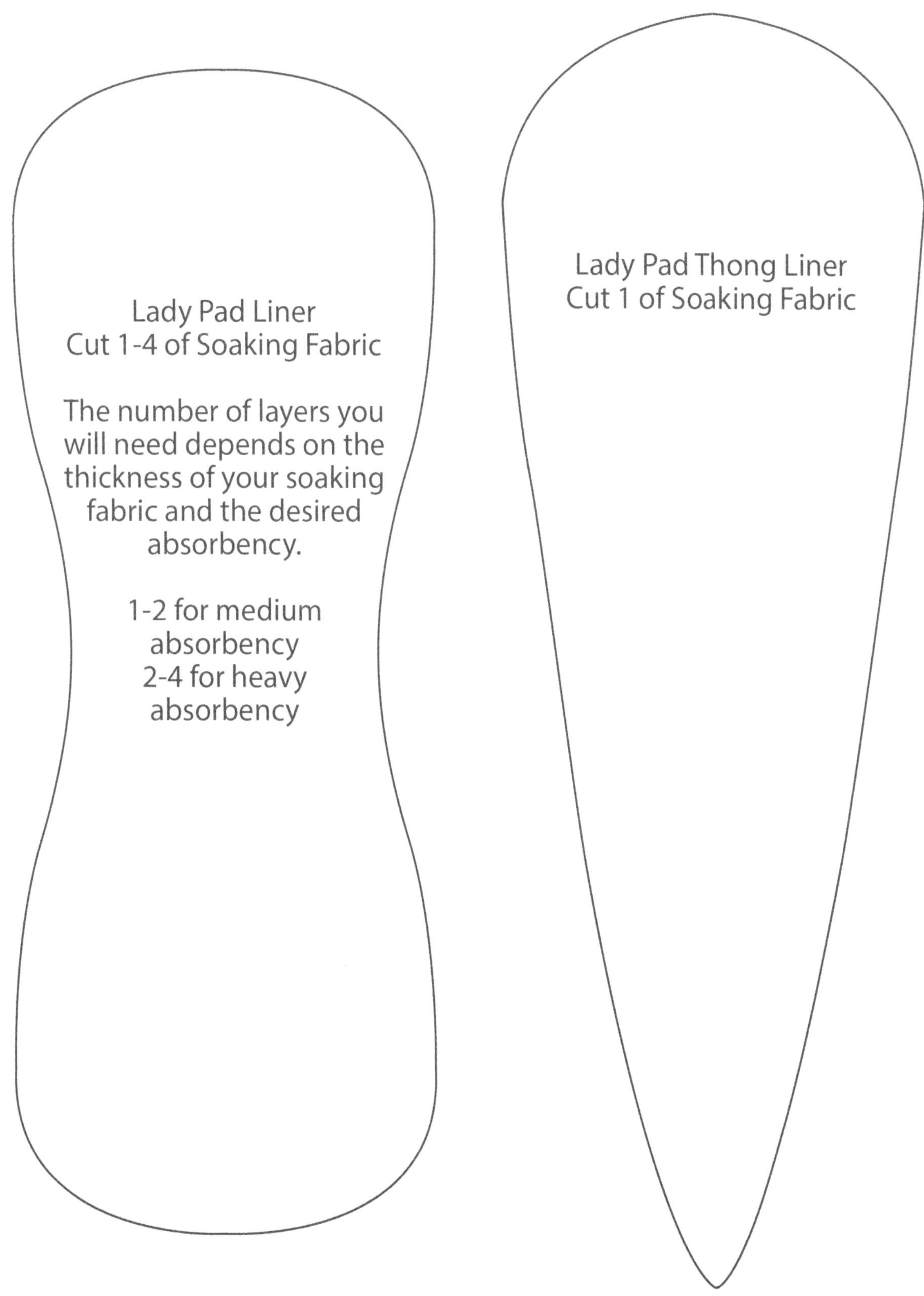
Lady Pad Liner
Cut 1-4 of Soaking Fabric
The number of layers you will need depends on the thickness of your soaking fabric and the desired absorbency.
1-2 for medium absorbency
2-4 for heavy absorbency
Lady Pad Thong Liner
Cut 1 of Soaking Fabric

Lady Pad Long Liner
Cut 1-2 of Soaking Fabric

The number of layers you will need depends on the thickness of your soaking fabric and the desired absorbency.

1 for light absorbency
2 for heavy absorbency

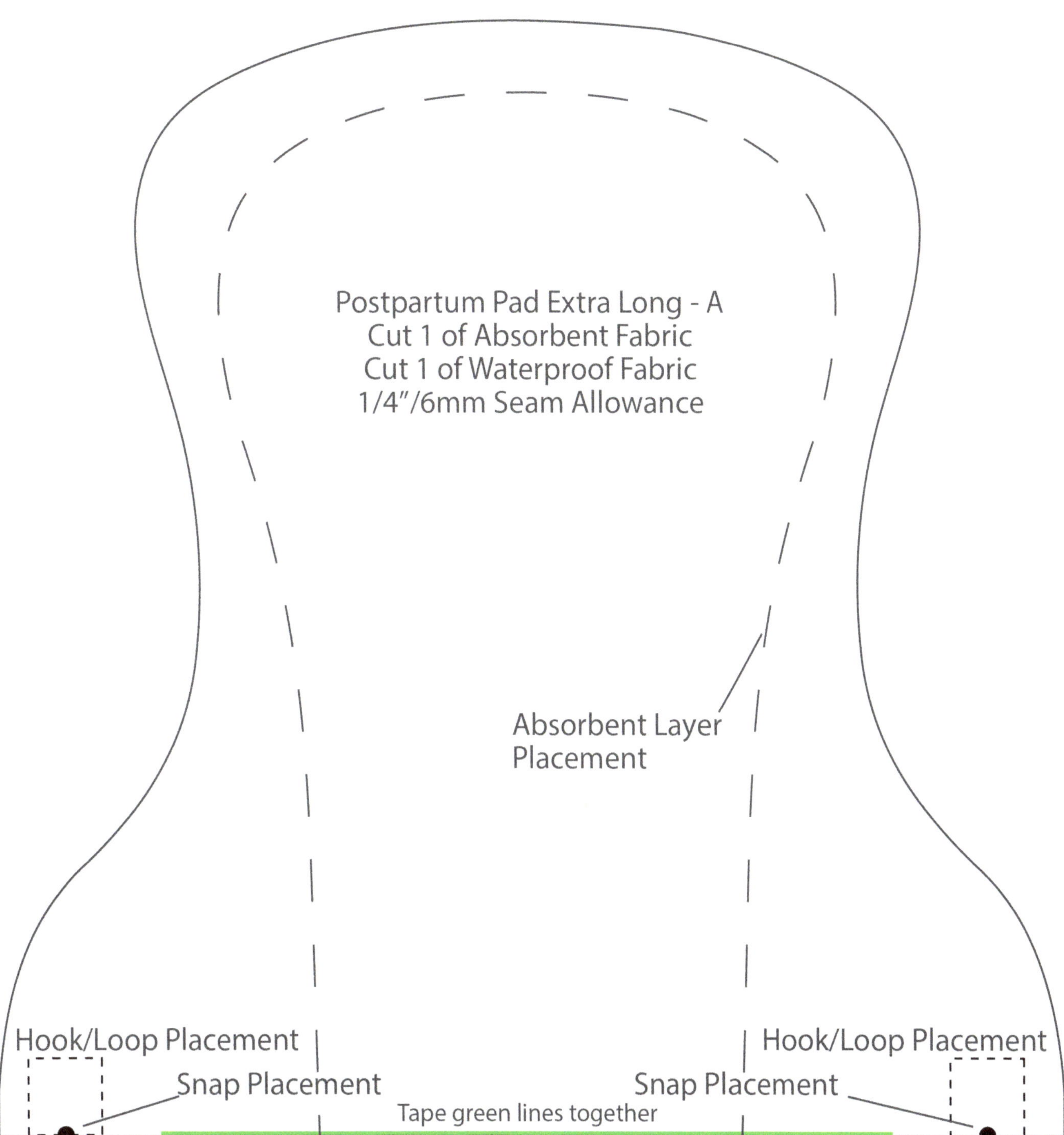
Postpartum Pad Extra Long - A
Cut 1 of Absorbent Fabric
Cut 1 of Waterproof Fabric
1/4"/6mm Seam Allowance
Absorbent Layer
Placement
Hook/Loop Placement
Hook/Loop Placement
Snap Placement
Snap Placement
Tape green lines together

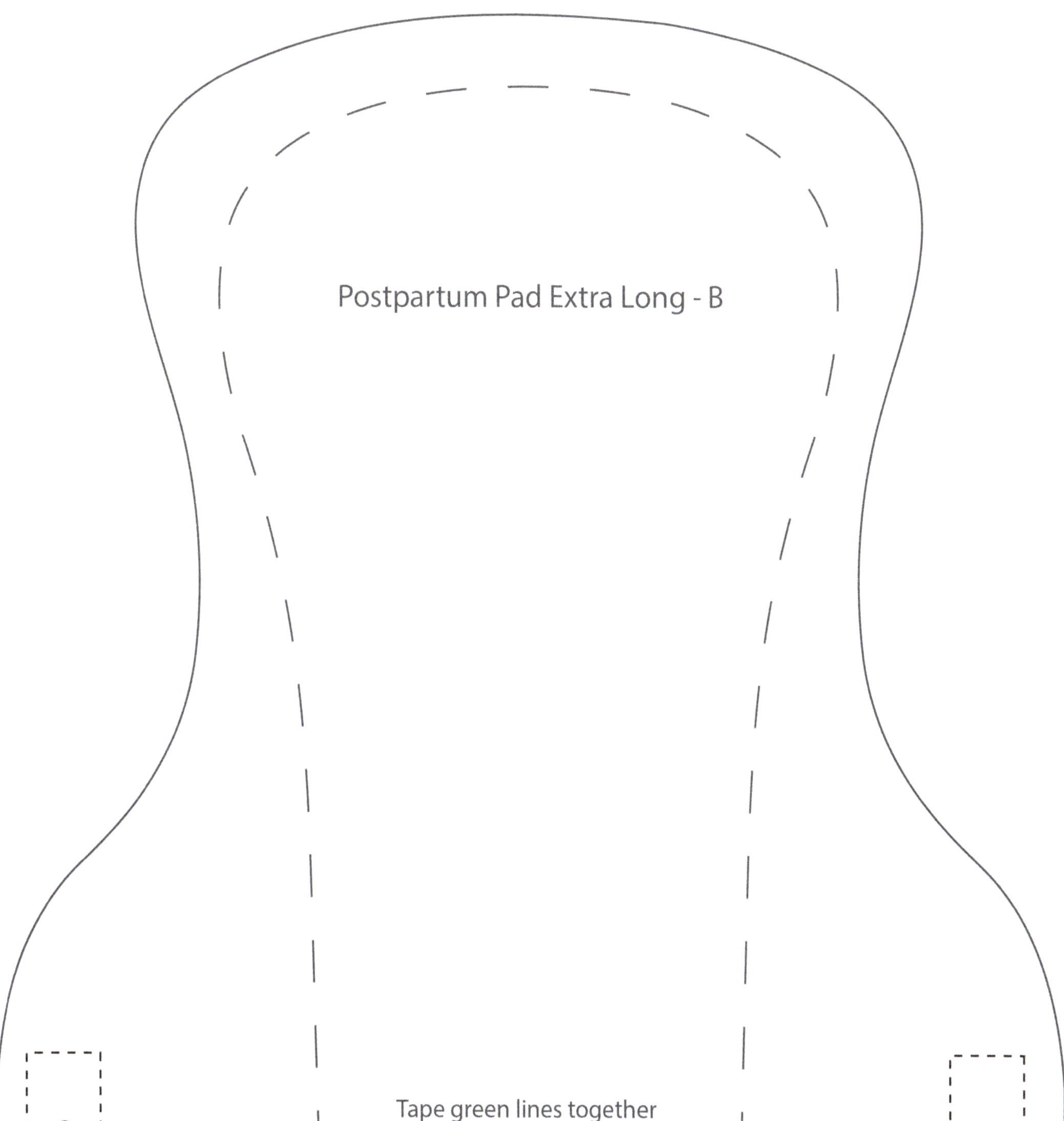
Postpartum Pad Extra Long - B
Tape green lines together

Lady Pad Long Liner - A
Cut 1-2 of Soaking Fabric

The number of layers you will need depends on the thickness of your soaking fabric and the desired absorbency.

1 for light absorbency
2 for heavy absorbency

Tape pink lines together

Tape pink lines together

Lady Pad Long Liner - B

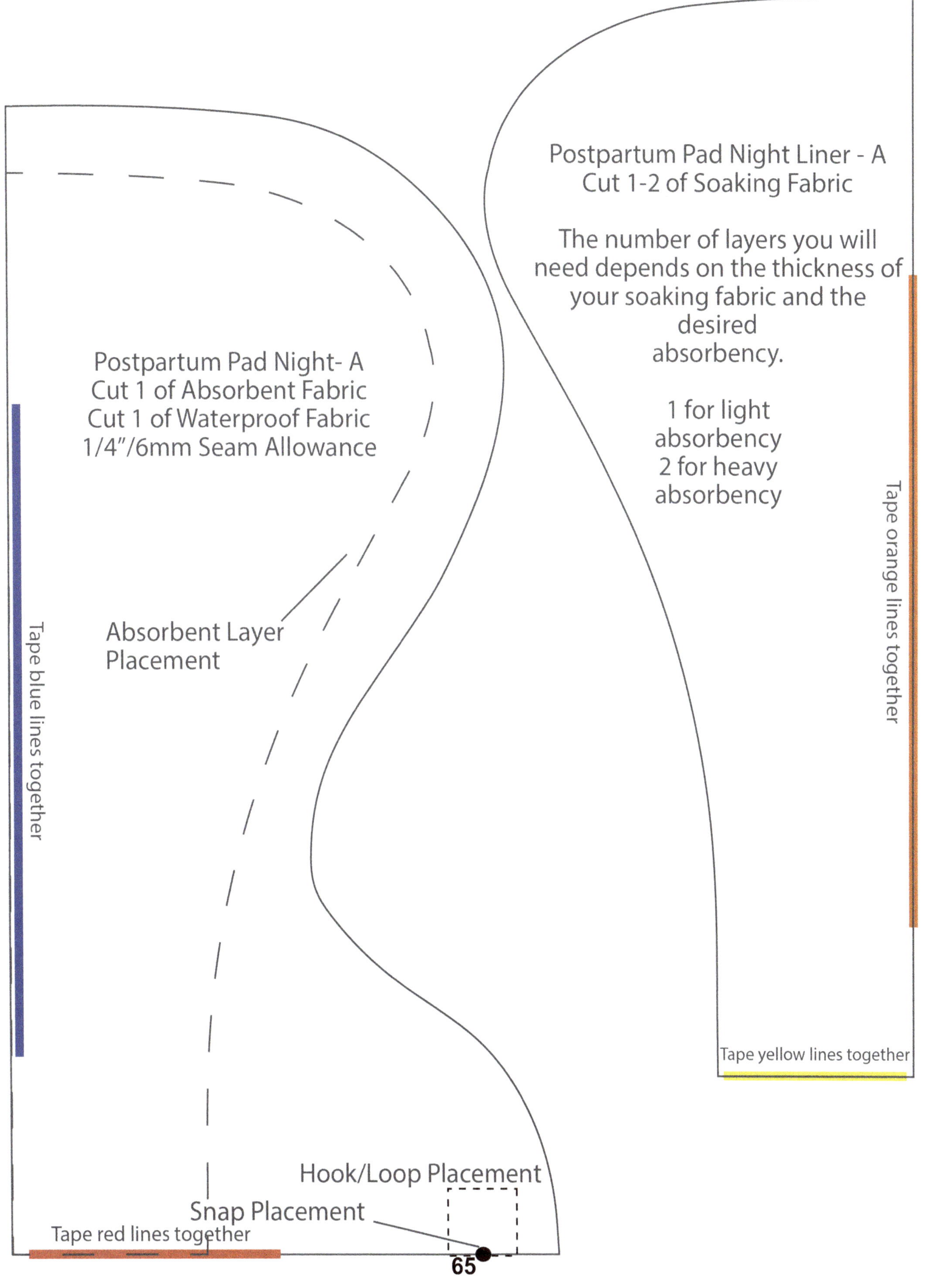
Postpartum Pad Night- A
Cut 1 of Absorbent Fabric
Cut 1 of Waterproof Fabric
1/4"/6mm Seam Allowance
Absorbent Layer Placement
Tape blue lines together
Hook/Loop Placement
Snap Placement
Tape red lines together
Postpartum Pad Night Liner - A
Cut 1-2 of Soaking Fabric
The number of layers you will need depends on the thickness of your soaking fabric and the desired absorbency.
1 for light absorbency
2 for heavy absorbency
Tape orange lines together
Tape yellow lines together

Postpartum Pad Night Liner - B

Tape orange lines together

Tape yellow lines together

Postpartum Pad Night - B

Tape blue lines together

Hook/Loop Placement

Snap Placement

Tape red lines together

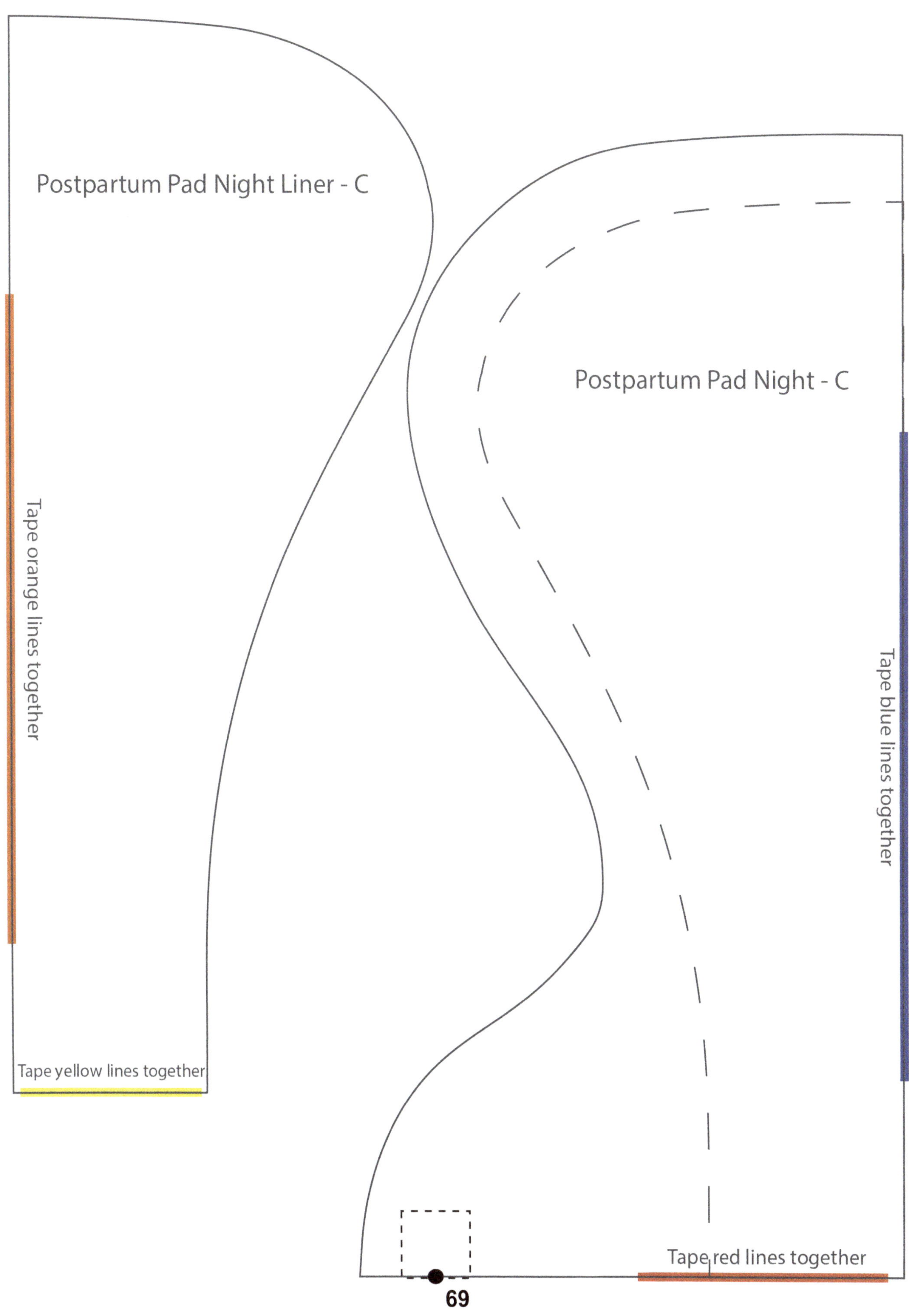
Postpartum Pad Night Liner - C
Tape orange lines together
Tape yellow lines together
Postpartum Pad Night - C
Tape blue lines together
Tape red lines together

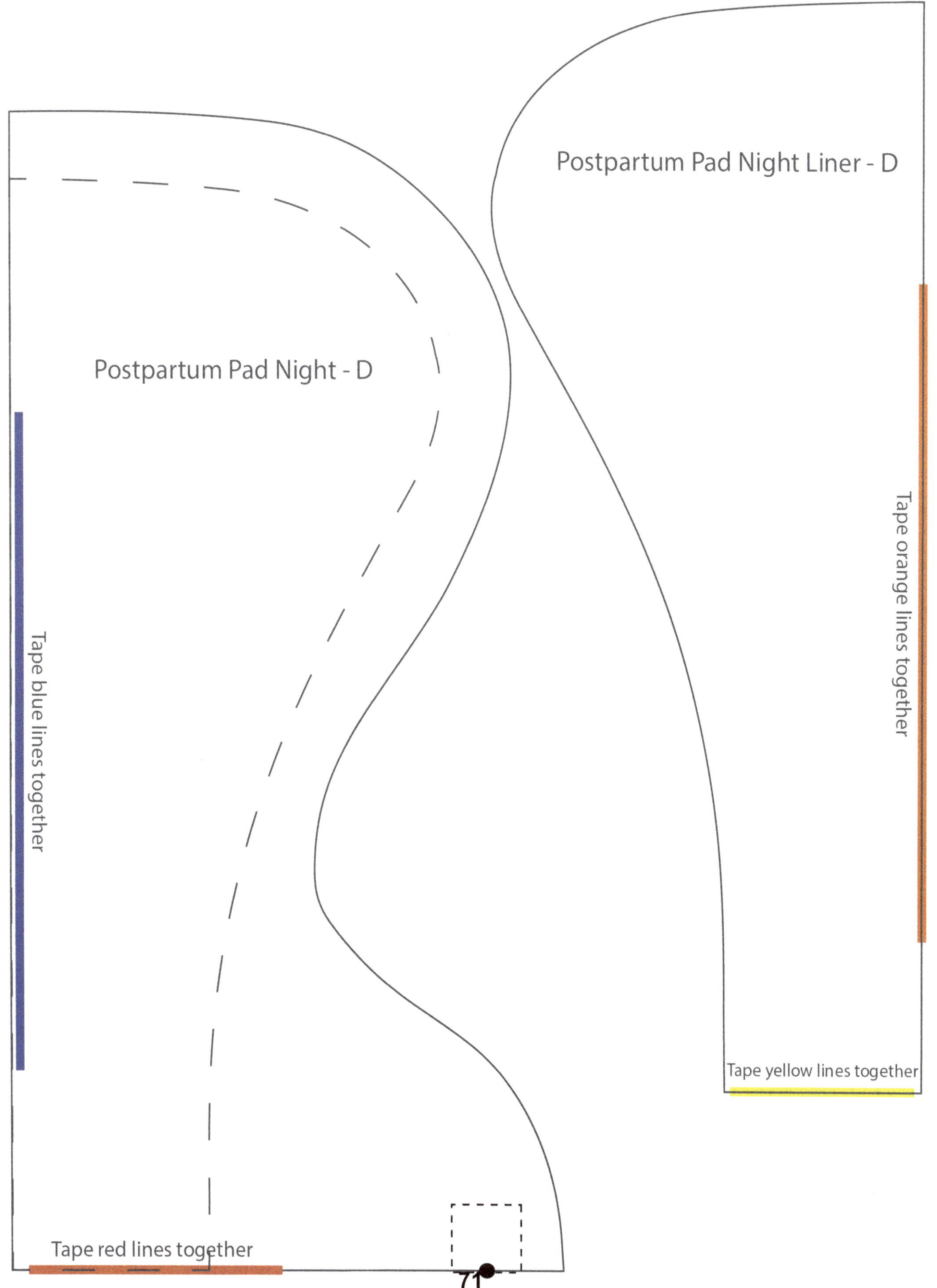
Postpartum Pad Night Liner - D
Postpartum Pad Night - D
Tape orange lines together
Tape blue lines together
Tape yellow lines together
Tape red lines together

Nursing Pads/Facial Wipes Pattern

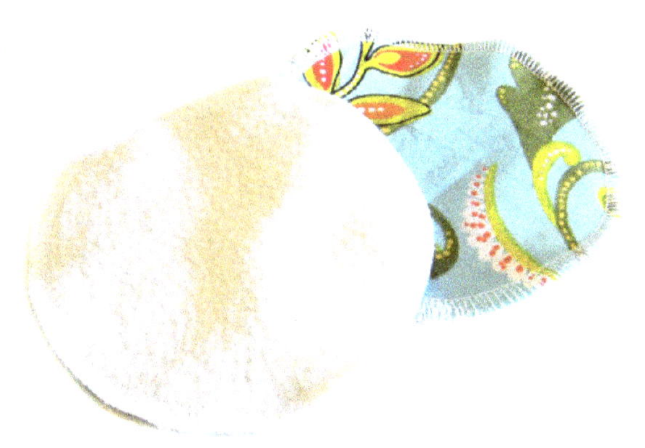

Materials:
- Scissors
- Sewing Machine with zig zag stitch or serger
- Thread
- Cotton Fabric
- Waterproof Lining Fabric
- Absorbent Fabric

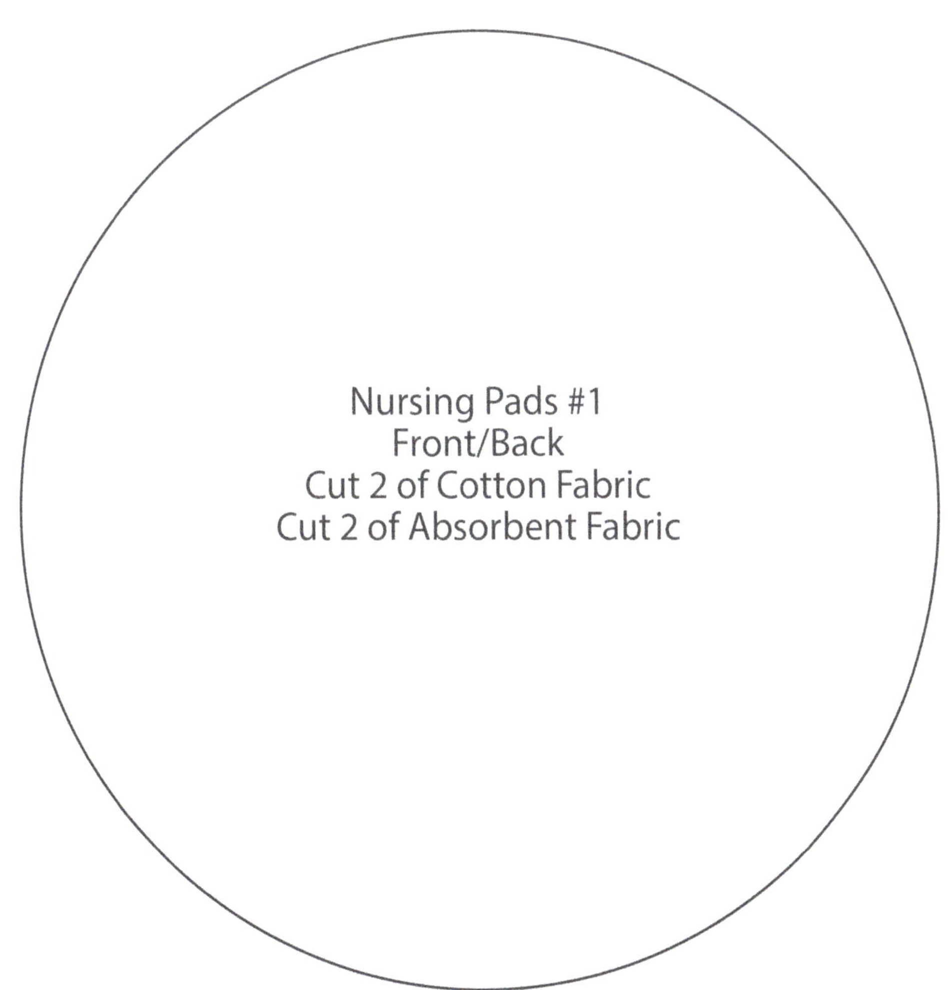

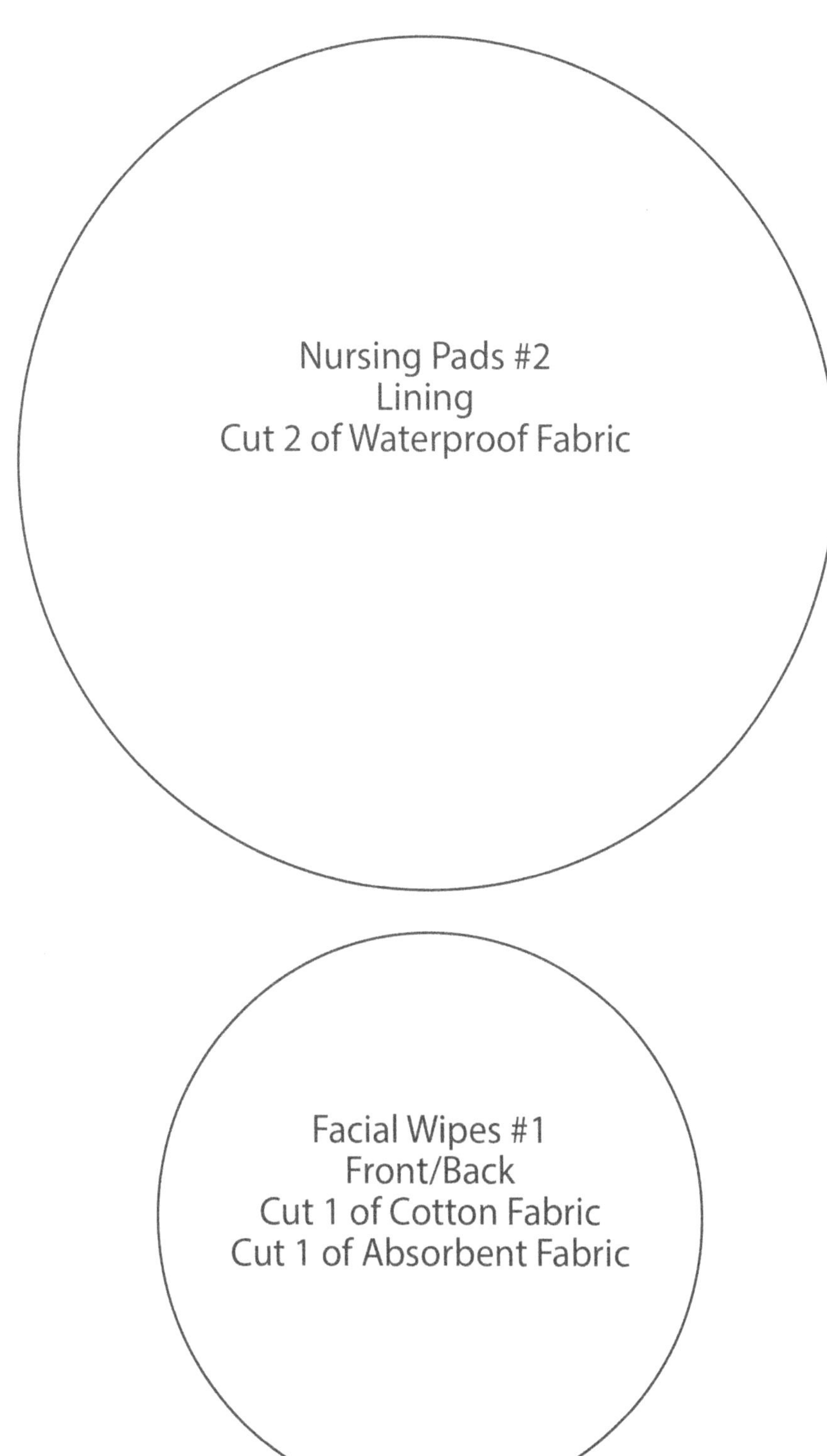
Nursing Pads #2
Lining
Cut 2 of Waterproof Fabric
Facial Wipes #1
Front/Back
Cut 1 of Cotton Fabric
Cut 1 of Absorbent Fabric

Lady Pad/Nursing Pads/ Facial Wipes Tutorial

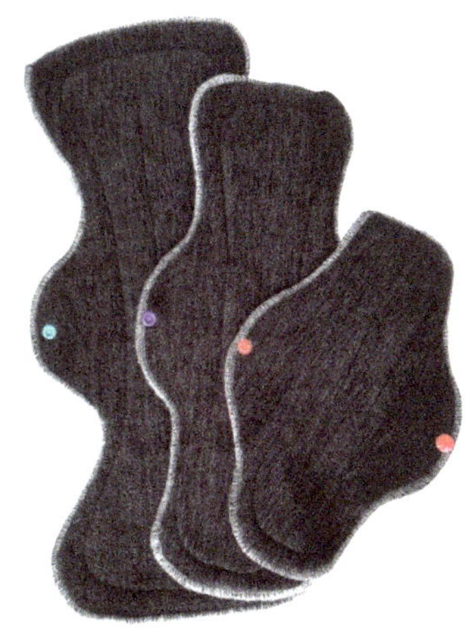

Step 1

-Wash your shrinkable fabrics in hot water to shrink the fabric before cutting.

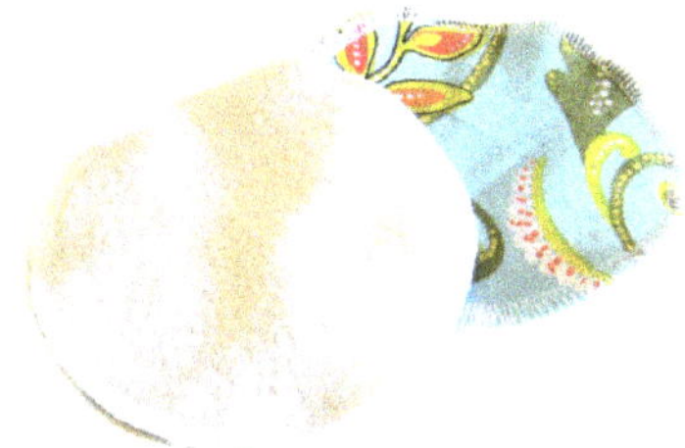

Step 2

-Cut patterns out in desired materials and mark all placement lines.

Step 3

-Layer fabrics wrong sides together with liner layer/s in between. Pin the liner/s in place from the outside of the pad (do not sew your pins inside). Use a serger or zig zag stitch to sew around the perimeter of the pad.

Step 4

-Use a straight stitch to sew through all layers. Stitch 1/4"/6mm around the inside perimeter of the liner/s to secure the liner/s in place.

Step 5

-Attach snaps or hook & loop where pattern indicates.perimeter of the liner/s to secure the liner/s in place.

Step 6

-Wash pads before use. *Please follow wash/dry instructions for the particular fabrics you choose. Do not use fabric softeners as they will cause a decrease in absorbency. If you are using waterproof PUL run your pads through a hot drying cycle (if your PUL wash/dry instructions permit using a dryer). The heat will close the needle holes making the pad more waterproof.

Passport Wallet Pattern

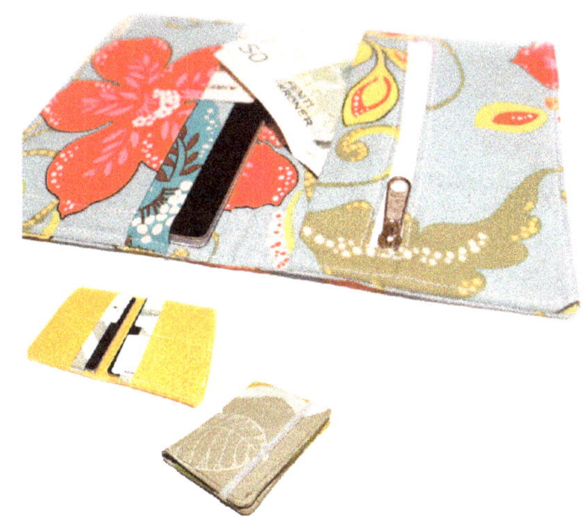

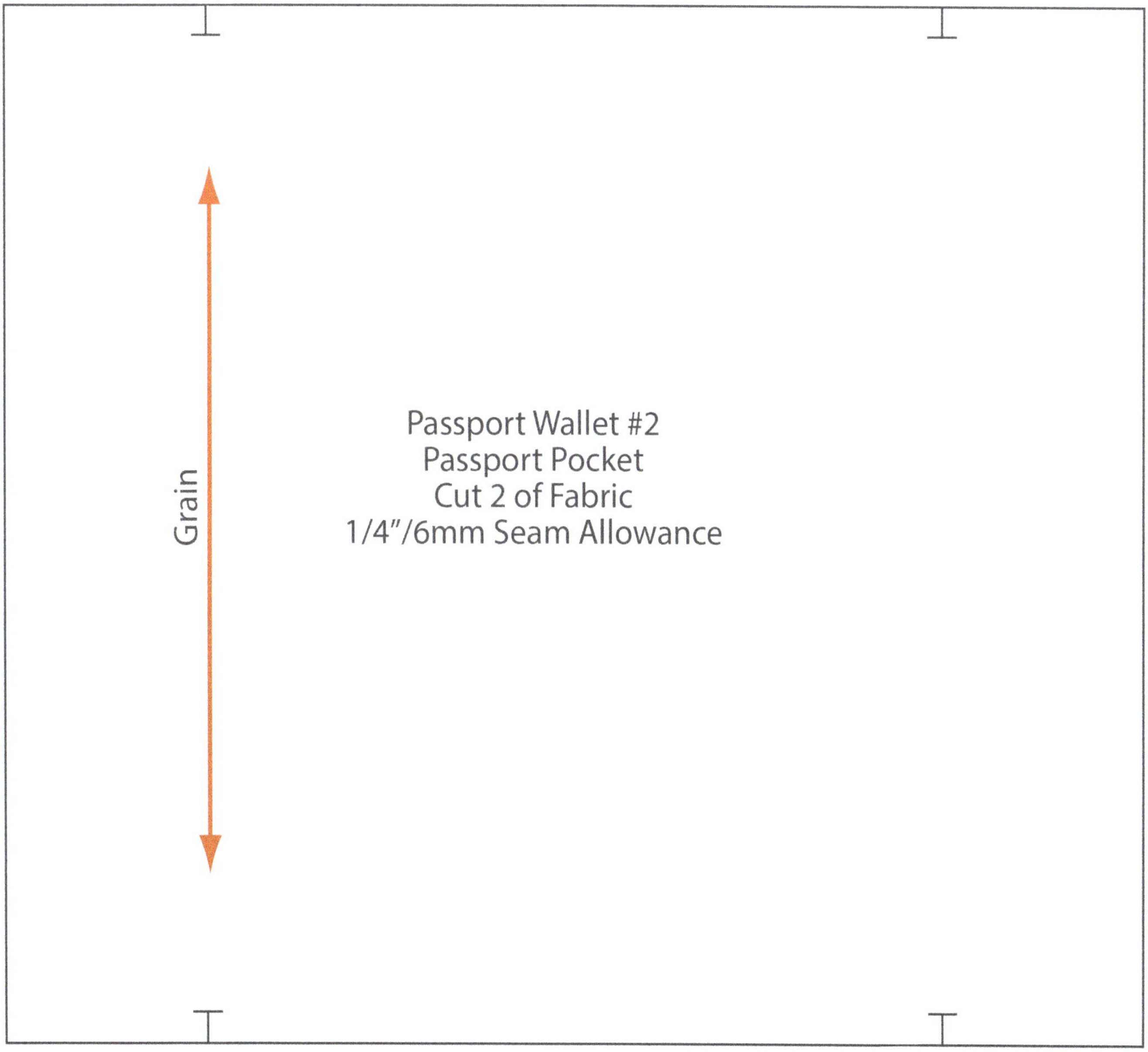

Grain

Passport Wallet #2
Passport Pocket
Cut 2 of Fabric
1/4"/6mm Seam Allowance

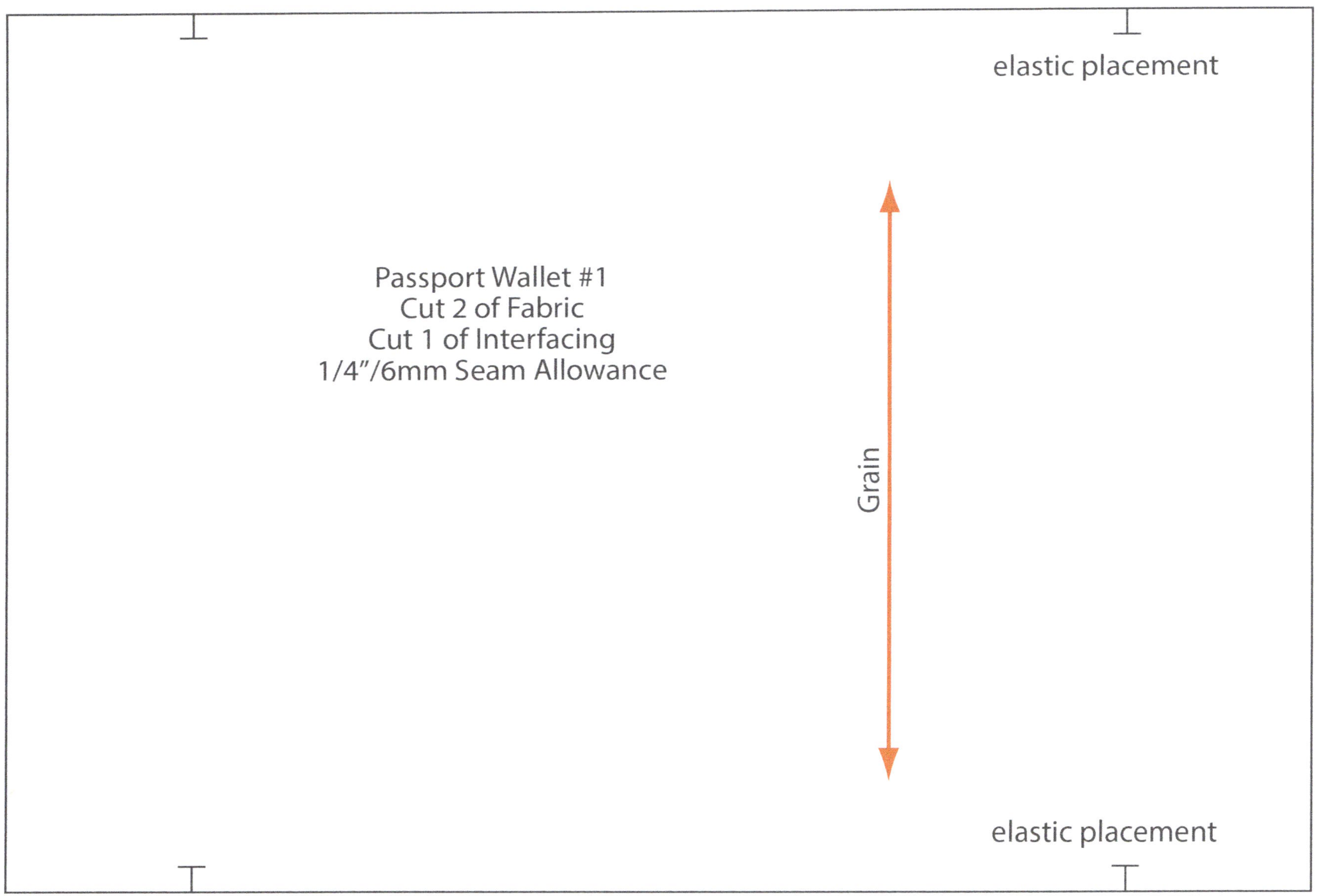
elastic placement
Passport Wallet #1
Cut 2 of Fabric
Cut 1 of Interfacing
1/4"/6mm Seam Allowance
Grain
elastic placement

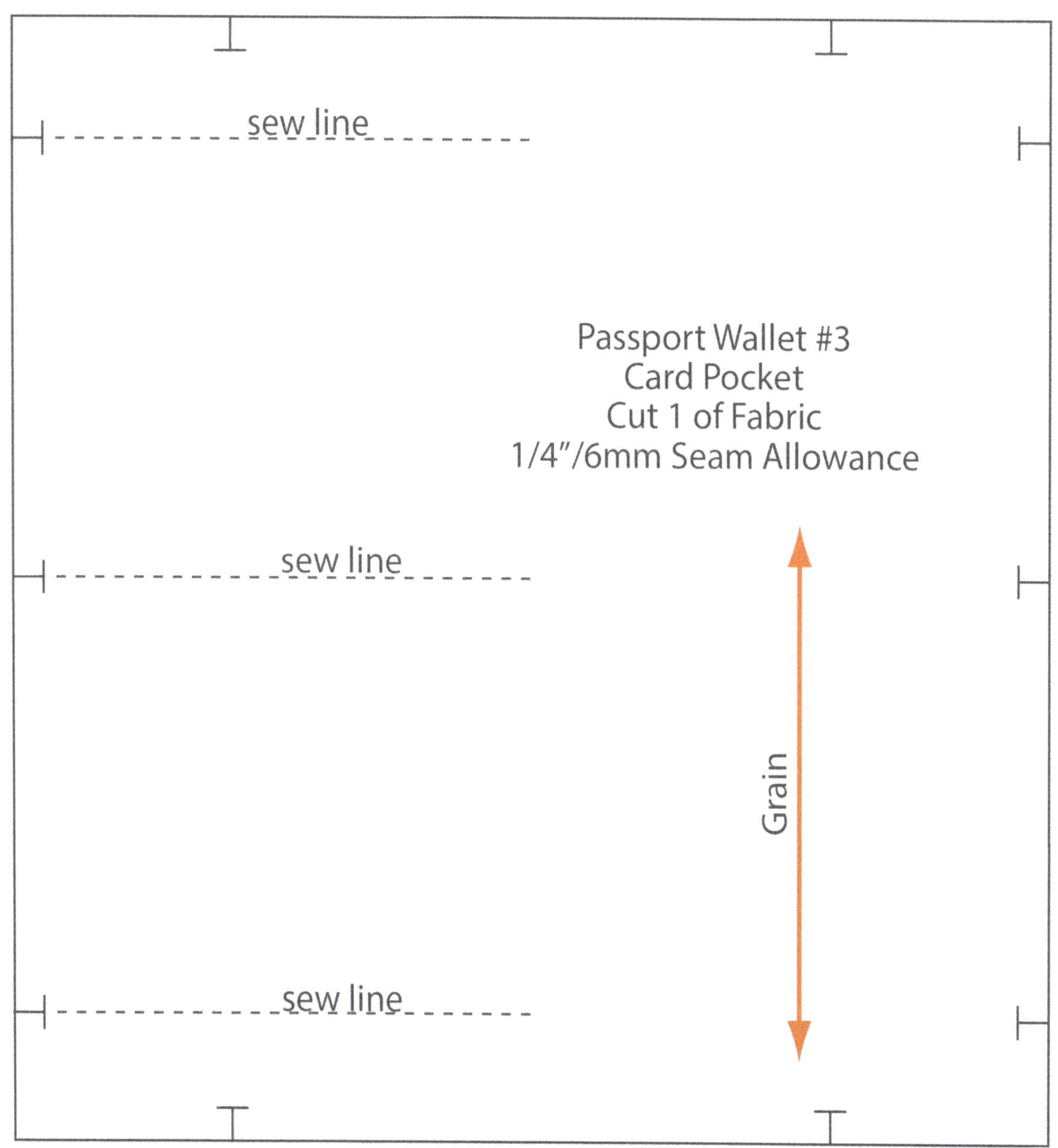
sew line
Passport Wallet #3
Card Pocket
Cut 1 of Fabric
1/4"/6mm Seam Allowance
sew line
Grain
sew line

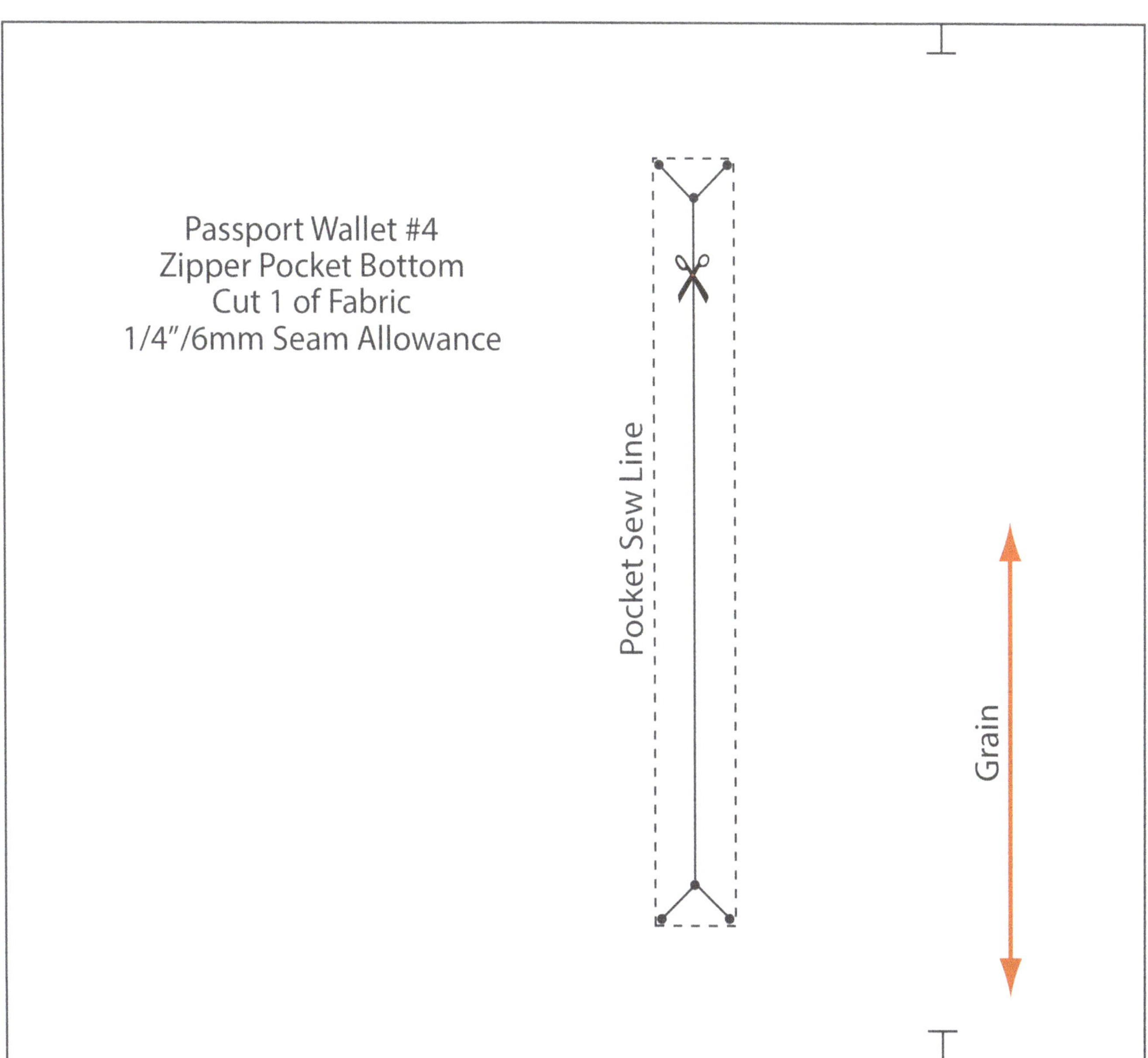
Passport Wallet #4
Zipper Pocket Bottom
Cut 1 of Fabric
1/4"/6mm Seam Allowance
Pocket Sew Line
Grain

Passport Wallet Tutorial

Materials:
-Base fabric
-Interfacing
-5"/14cm Zipper
-6"/15cm Elastic

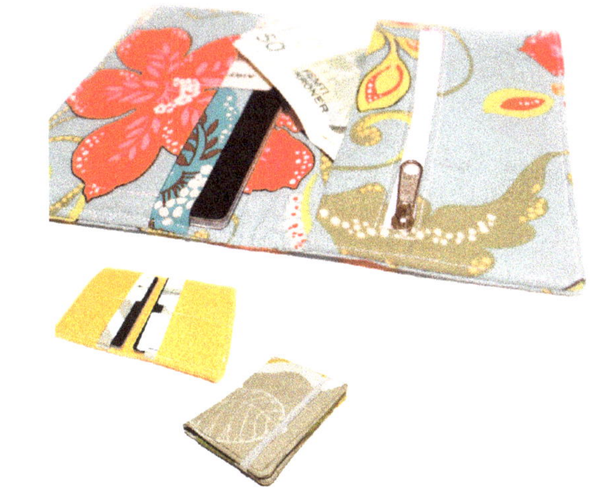

Step 1

-Cut out the patterns.

Step 2

-Position the pattern pieces on the fabric so the grain line runs parallel to the grain or selvage of the fabric. (If you have directional fabric as shown in photo with a clear top and bottom to the design place the grain line parallel to the design).

-Mark all notches, lines and dots on the fabric. Mark dots on zipper pocket piece #4 on the wrong side of the fabric.

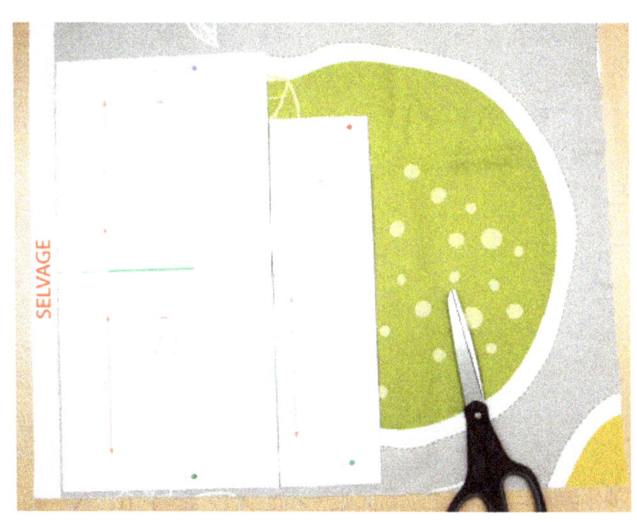

Step 3

-Iron or sew the interfacing onto one piece of #1 according to the manufacturer's instructions.

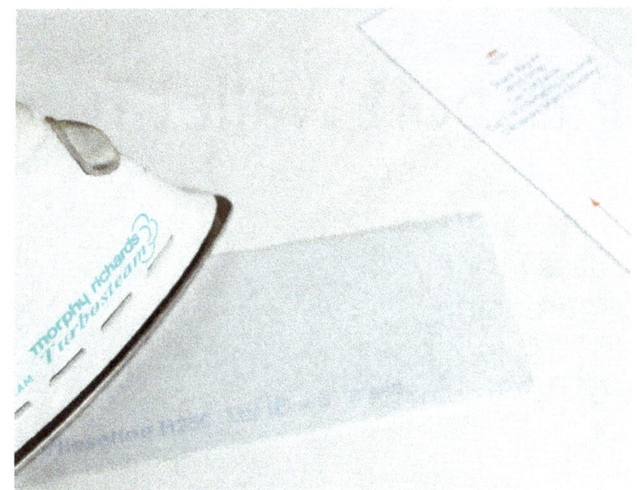

Step 4

-Make the card pocket

-Fold one piece of #2 and card pocket #3 in half parallel to the grain line matching the notches and iron.

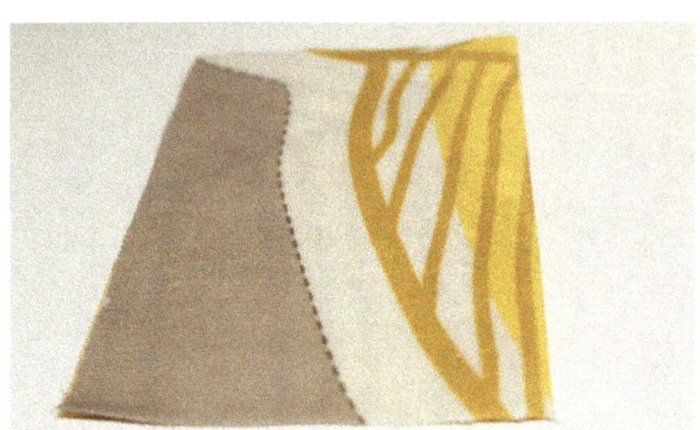

-Pin card pocket on top of passport pocket.

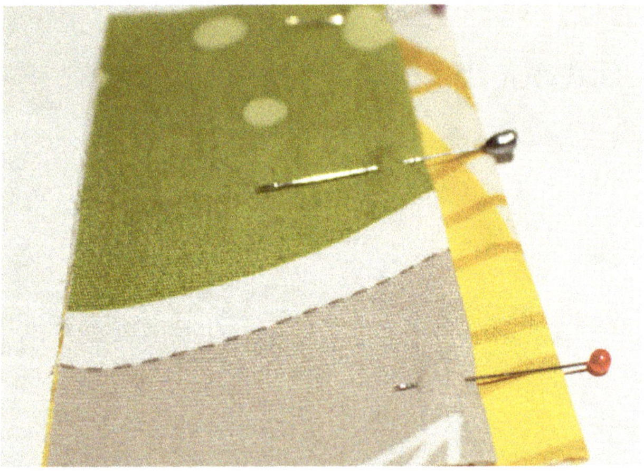

-Sew along the lines indicated by the pattern to form 2 card pockets.

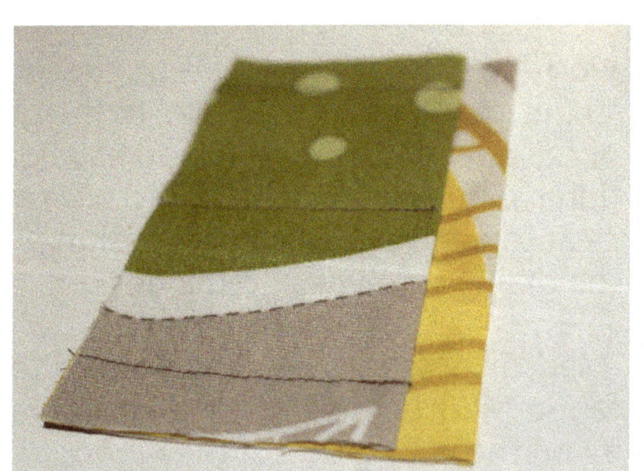

-Test out the pockets to make sure your cards fit.

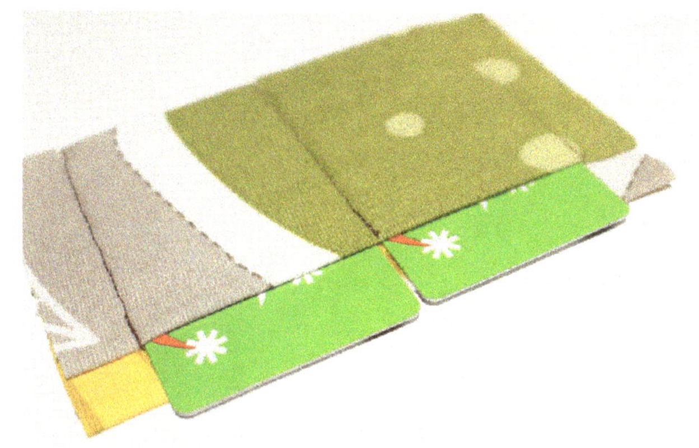

Step 5

-Make the zipper pocket.

-Place zipper pocket on top of passport pocket right sides together.

-Stitch along sew lines as indicated on the pattern being careful to stitch as close to a perfect rectangle as possible.

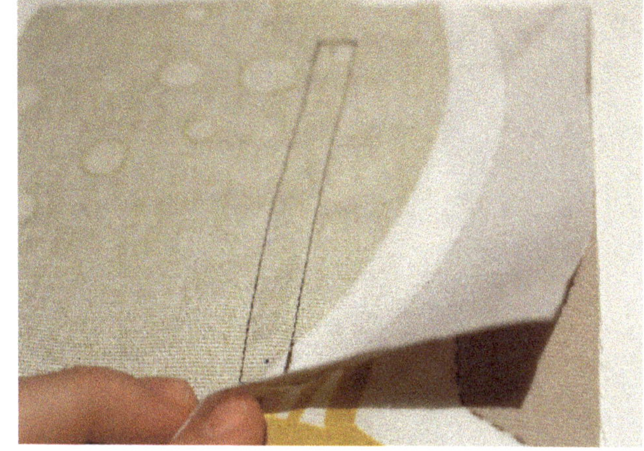

-Cut the opening along the scissor line as indicated on the pattern being careful to clip the corners as close to the stitching as possible without clipping past the stitching.

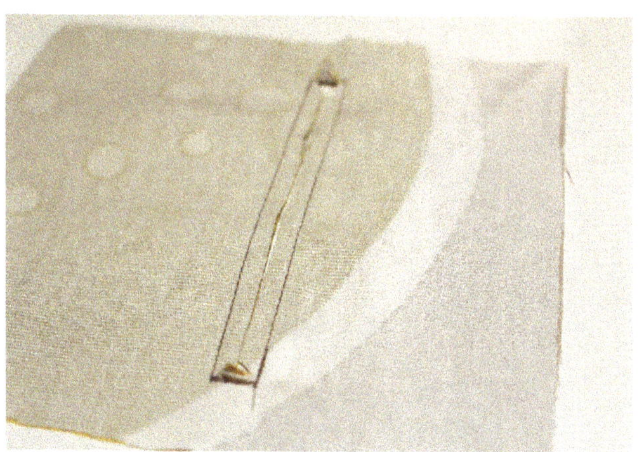

-Turn the pocket right sides out through the zipper hole.

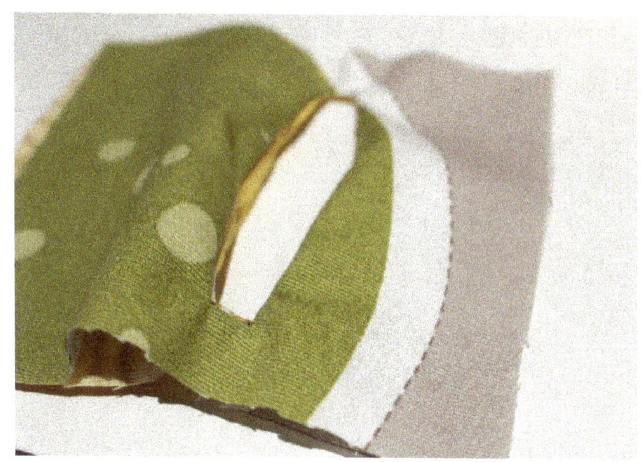

-Iron the opening flat

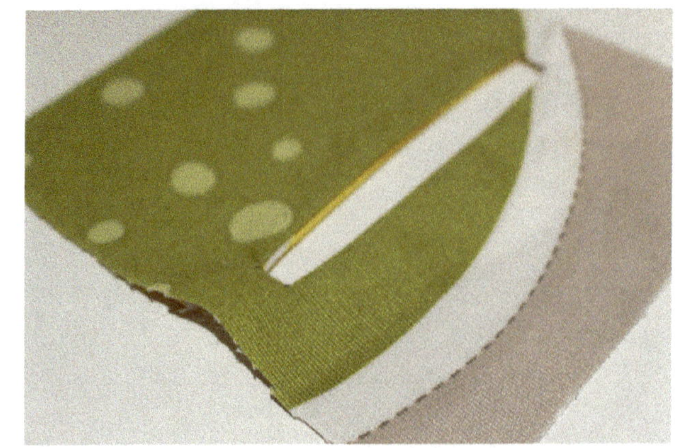

-Pin the zipper in place

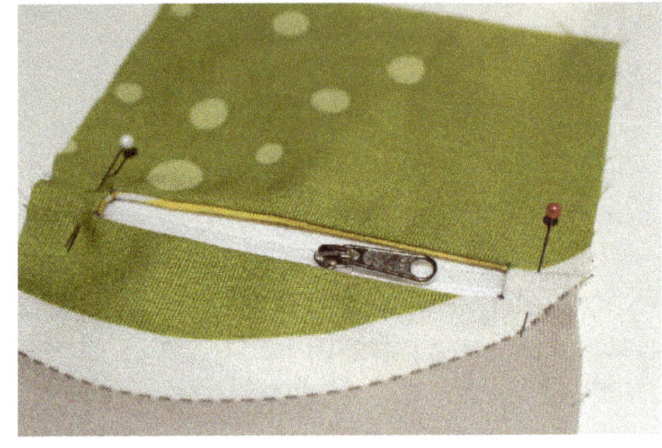

-Stitch around the entire edge of the opening

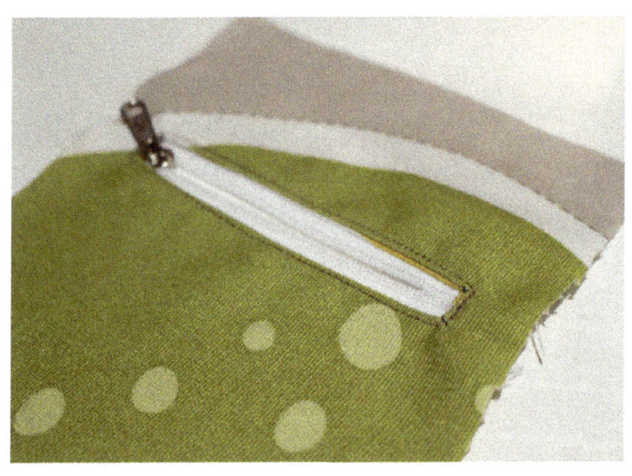

-Trim the edge of the zipper off close to the stitching

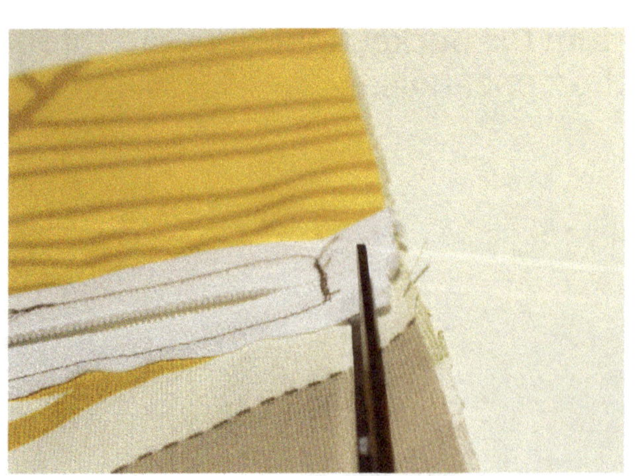

Step 6

-Assembling the wallet.

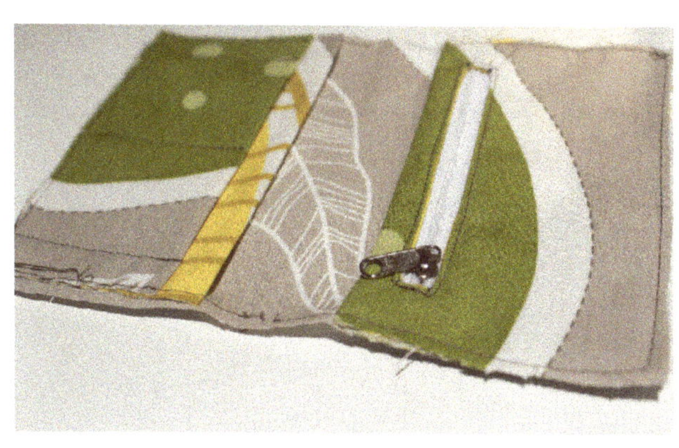

-Pin the two pockets in place on top of piece #1 without interfacing matching the corners and notches.

-Pin the elastic in place as indicated on the pattern.

-Baste stitch around the entire perimeter of the wallet using a scant seam allowance.

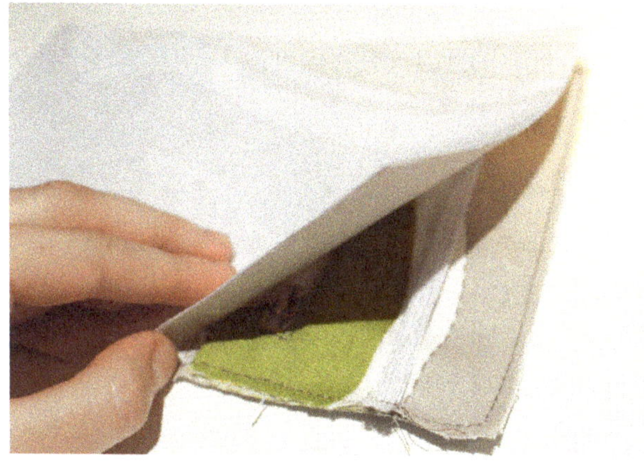

-Place the piece #1 with interfacing on top of wallet right sides together.

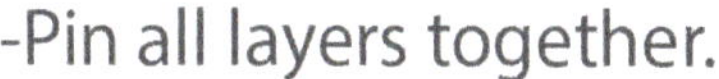

-Pin all layers together.

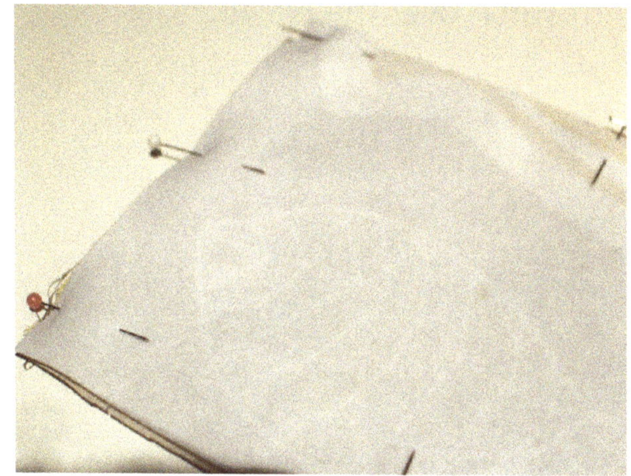

-Sew along outer perimeter leaving a gap on one side.

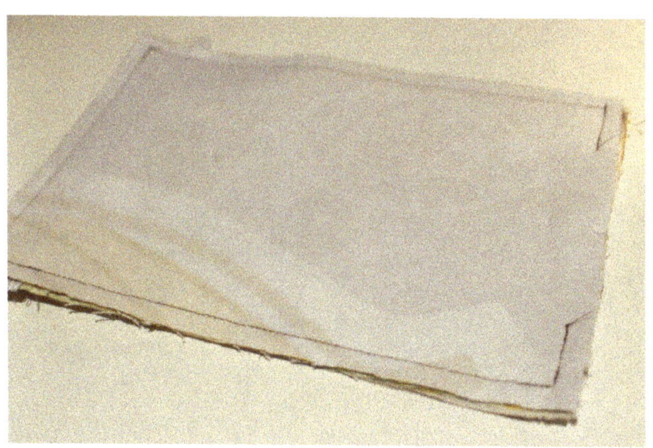

-Trim the four corners.

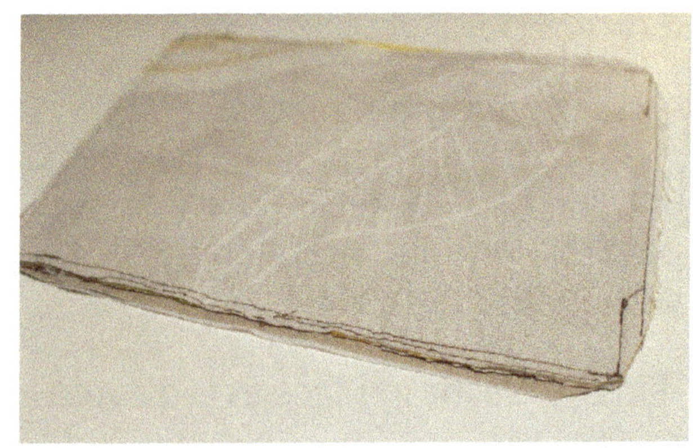

Step 7

-Turn the wallet right side out.

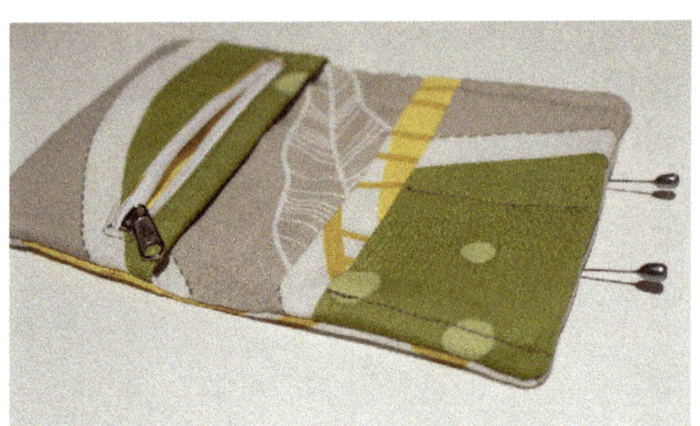

-Use the gap to turn the wallet right side out.

-Poke the corners out with a bone creaser.

-Pin the gap closed and iron the entire seam. Avoid using harsh heat against the zipper and the elastic.

-Top stitch around the entire perimeter. Do not stitch over the elastic.

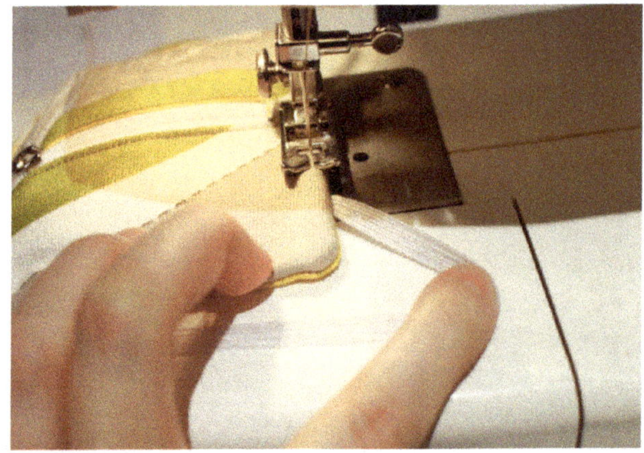

-The wallet is complete. Now go travel!

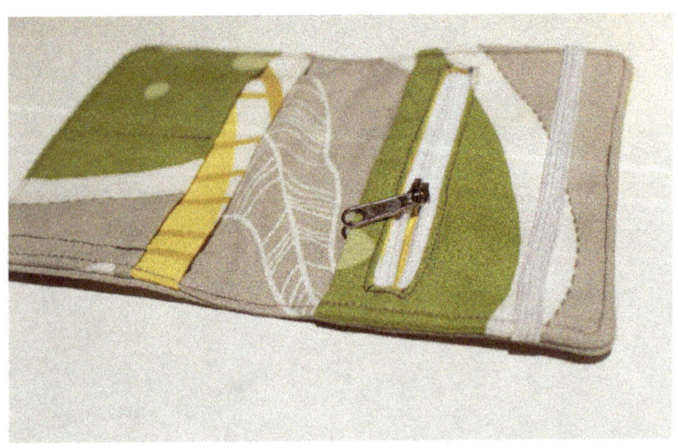

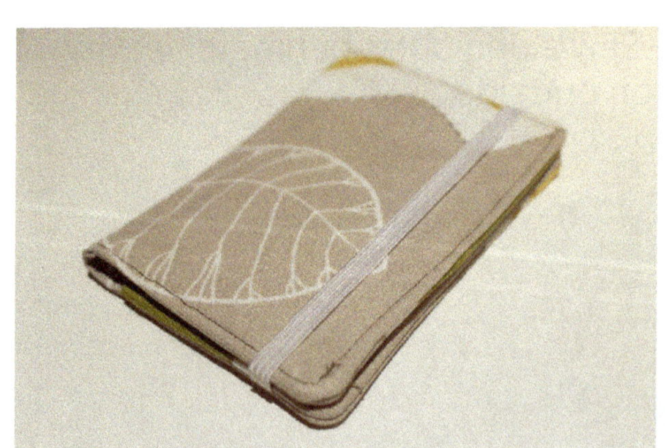

Snack Bag & Wet Bag Patterns

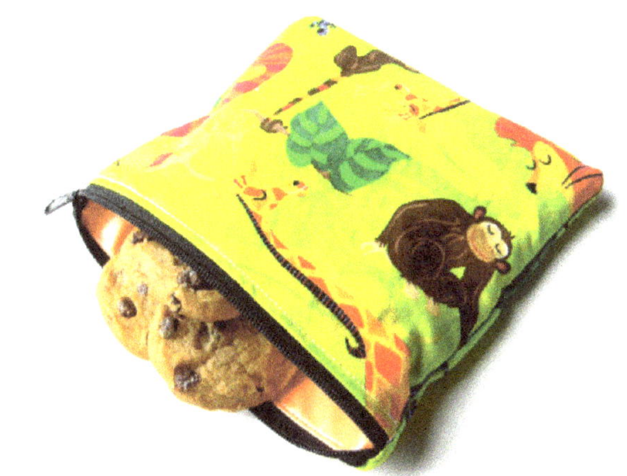

Grain

Bag #1-A
Sandwich Size
Cut 1 of Fabric
Cut 1 of Waterproof Fabric
1/4"/6mm Seam Allowance

Tape pink lines together

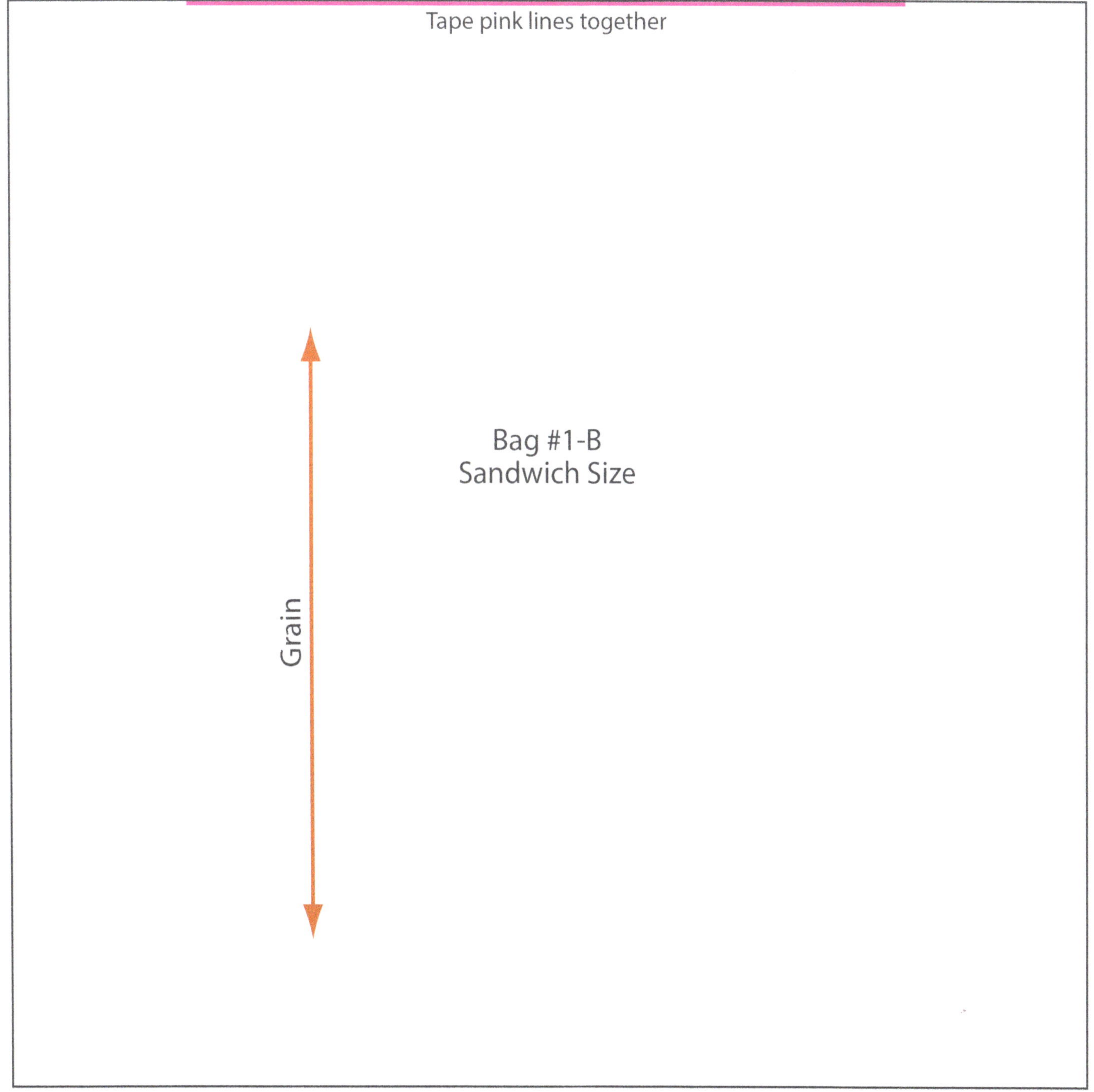
Tape pink lines together
Bag #1-B
Sandwich Size
Grain

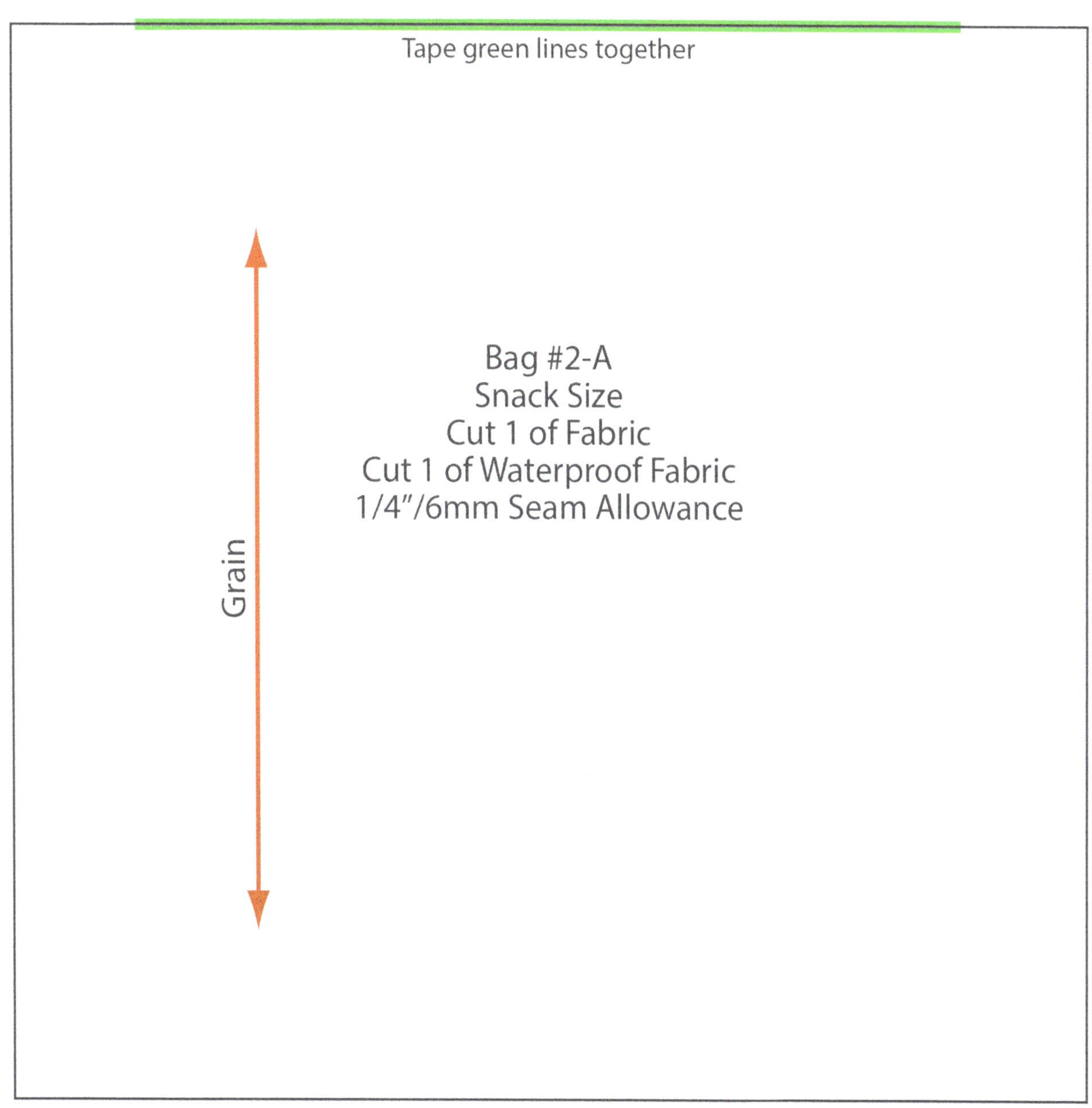
Tape green lines together
Bag #2-A
Snack Size
Cut 1 of Fabric
Cut 1 of Waterproof Fabric
1/4"/6mm Seam Allowance
Grain

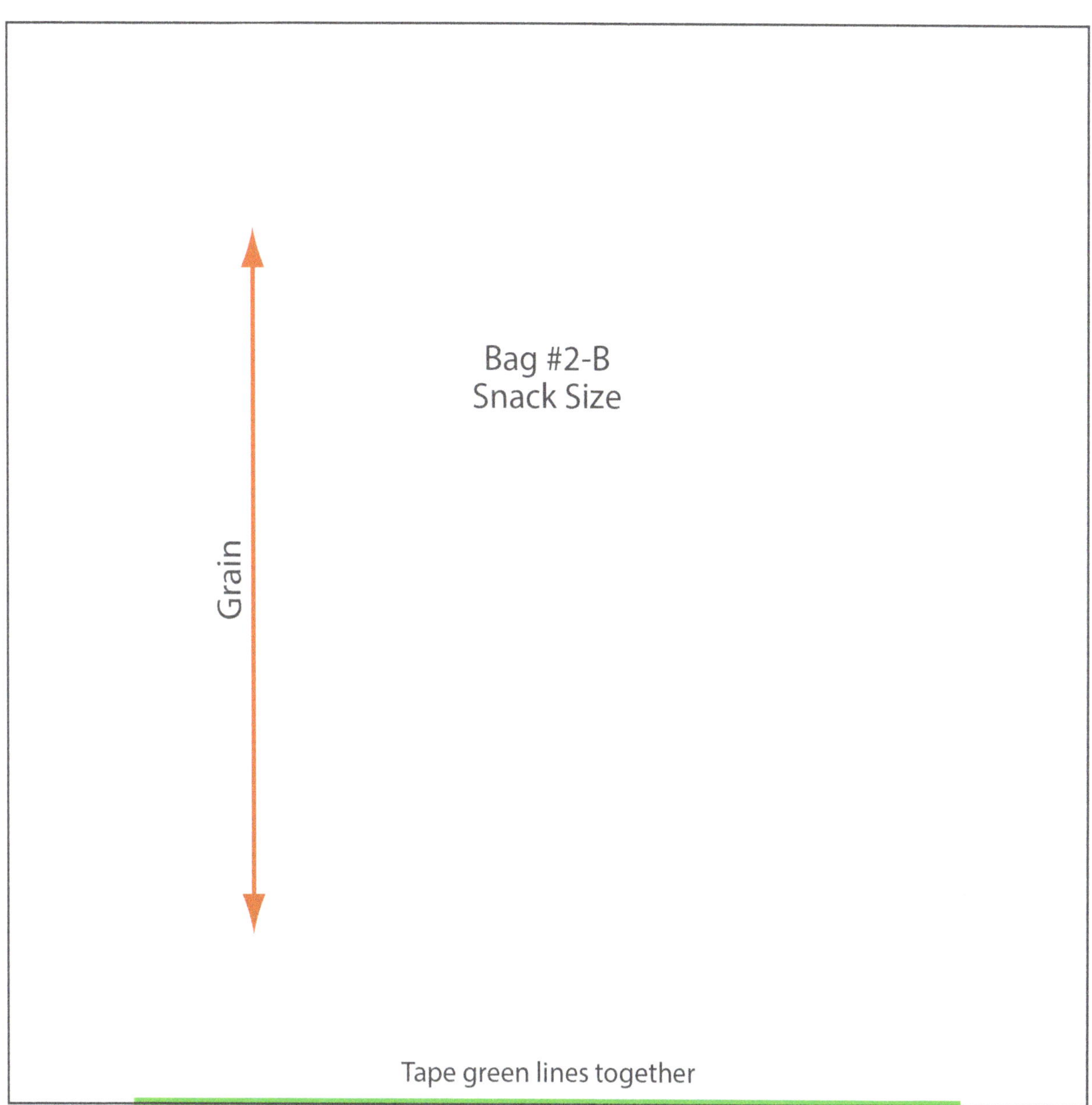
Bag #2-B
Snack Size
Grain
Tape green lines together

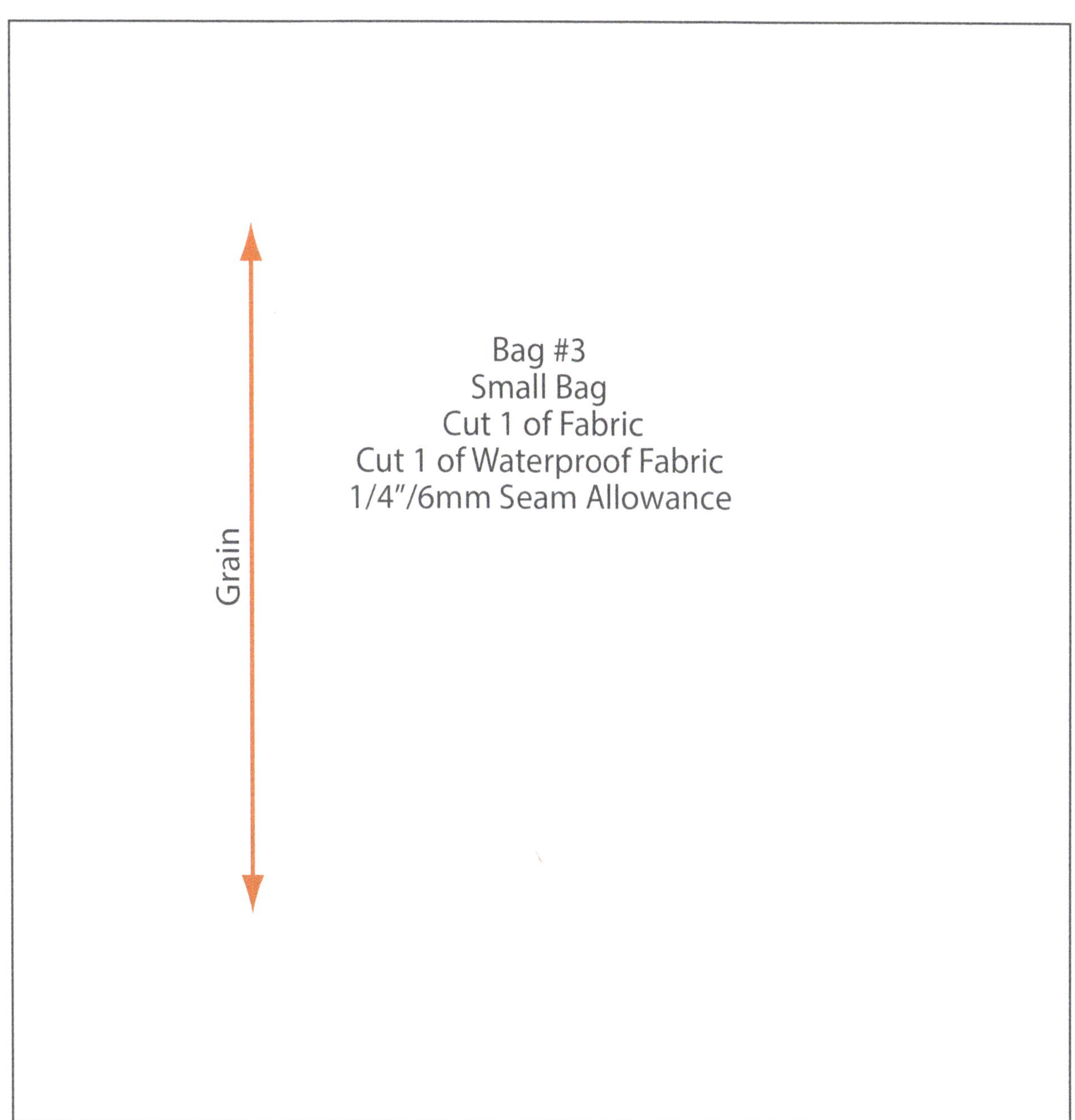
Bag #3
Small Bag
Cut 1 of Fabric
Cut 1 of Waterproof Fabric
1/4"/6mm Seam Allowance
Grain

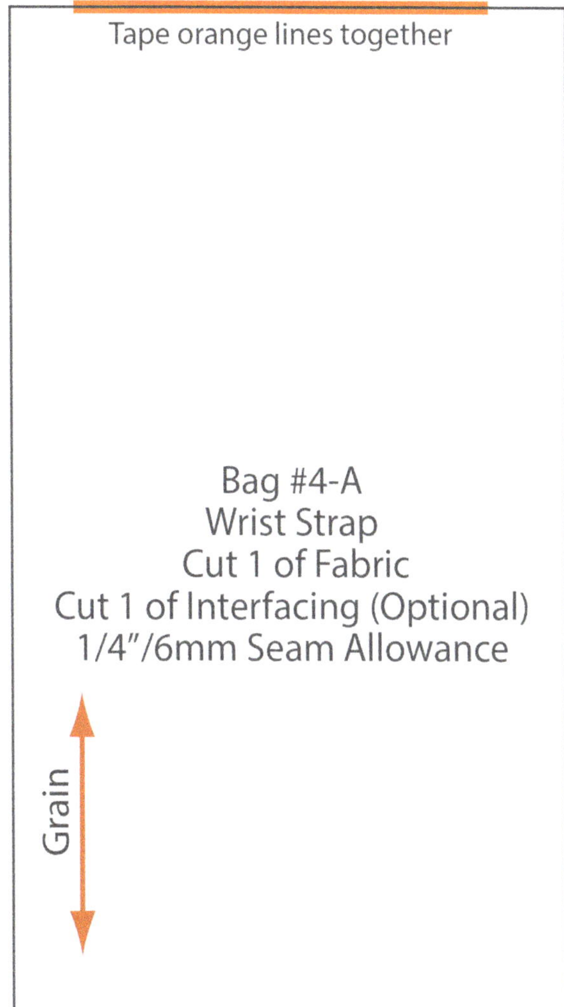
Tape orange lines together
Bag #4-A
Wrist Strap
Cut 1 of Fabric
Cut 1 of Interfacing (Optional)
1/4"/6mm Seam Allowance
Grain

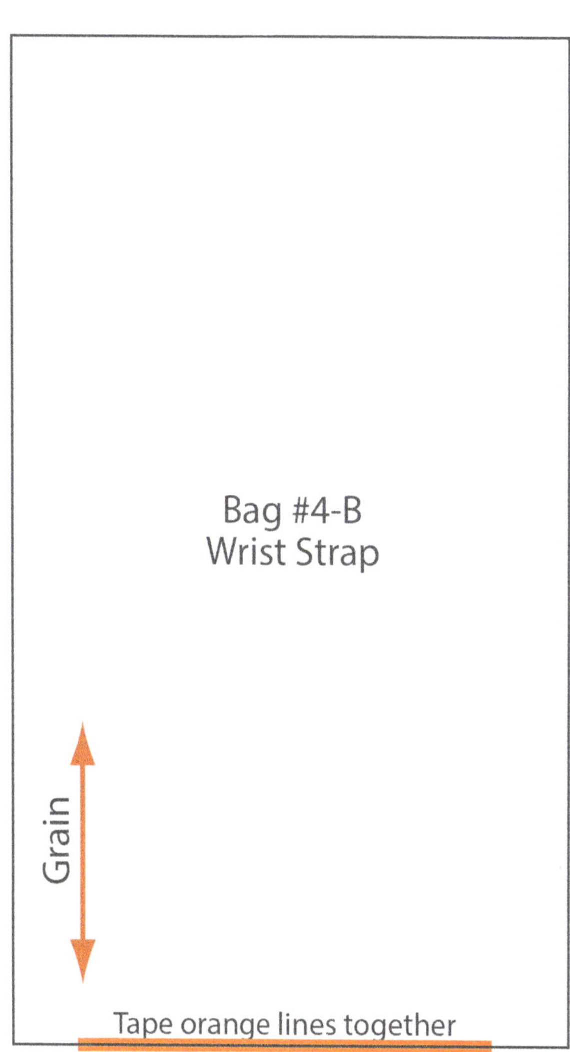
Bag #4-B
Wrist Strap
Grain
Tape orange lines together

Cut and tape pattern #5 together or cut out a rectangle on your fabric of 10.5″ x 29″, these are the final fabric measurements.

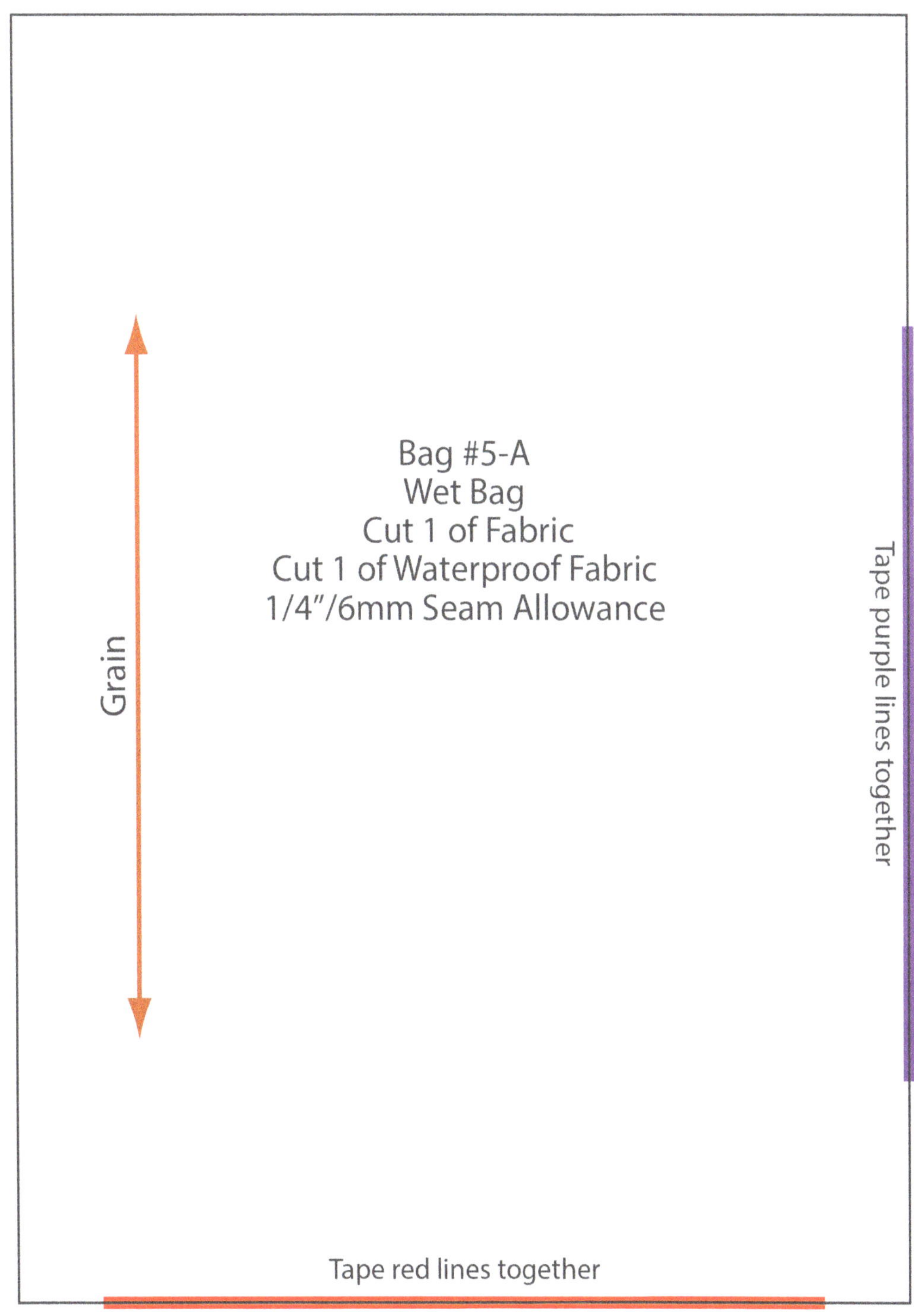

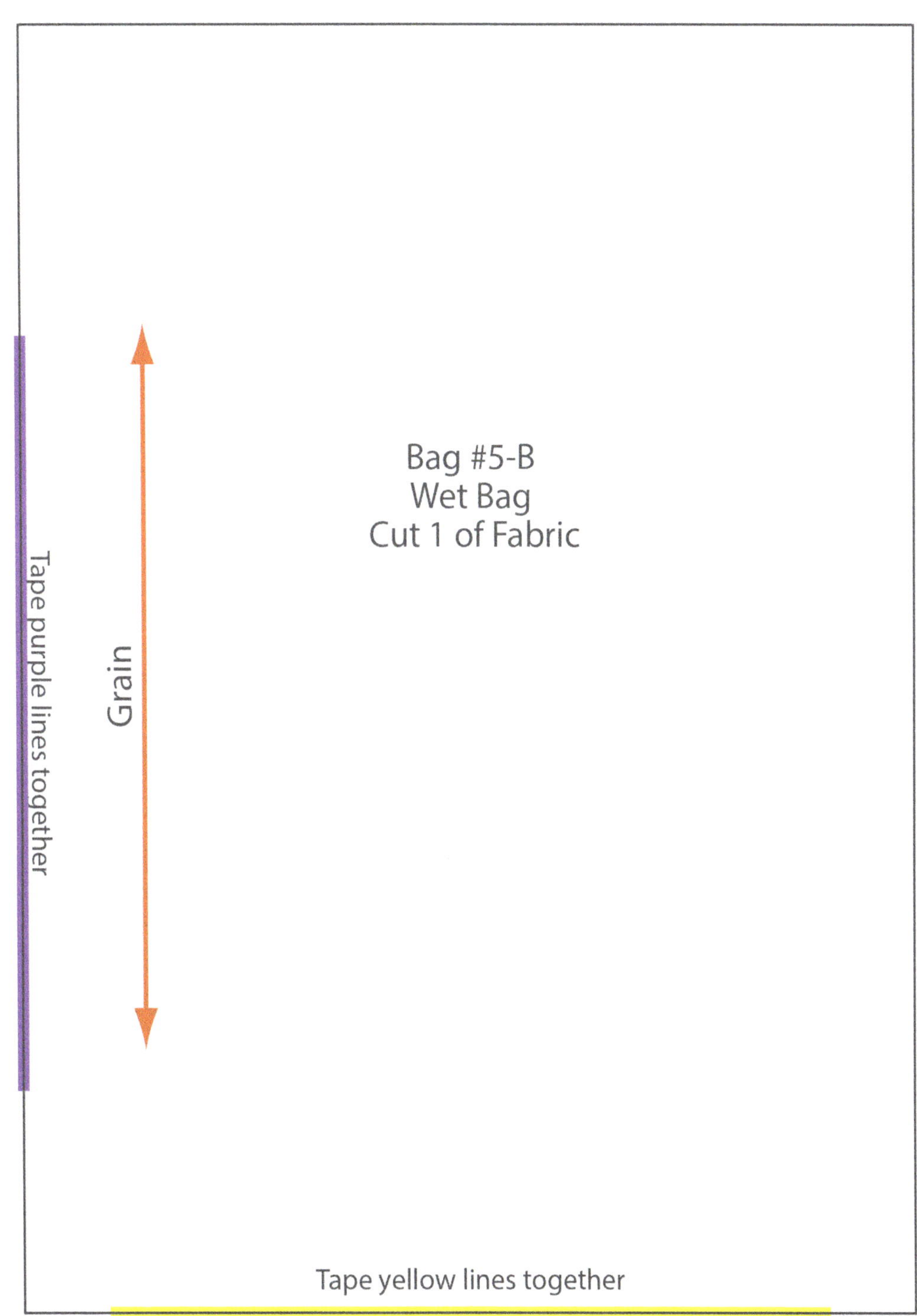
Bag #5-B
Wet Bag
Cut 1 of Fabric
Grain
Tape purple lines together
Tape yellow lines together

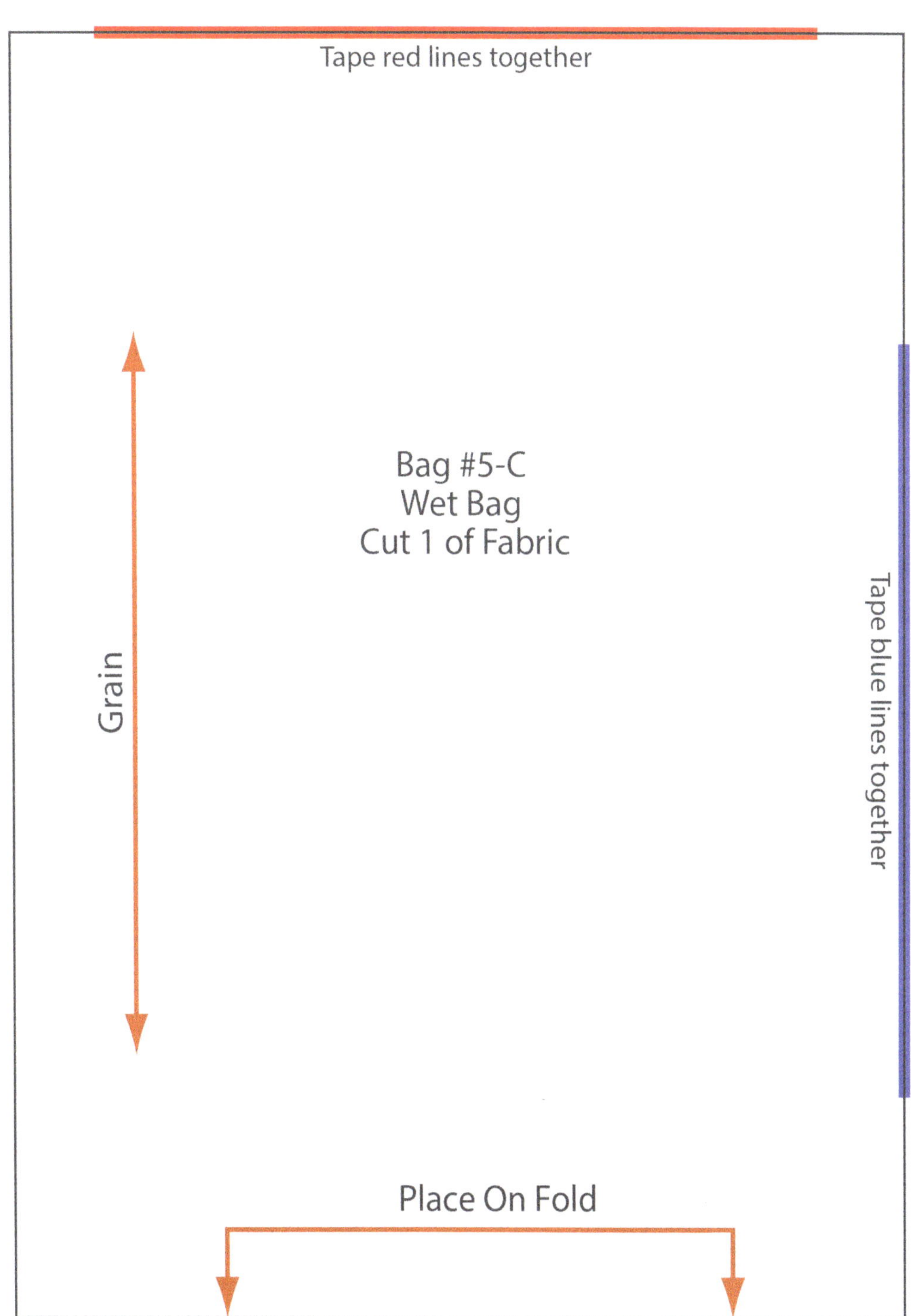
Tape red lines together
Bag #5-C
Wet Bag
Cut 1 of Fabric
Grain
Tape blue lines together
Place On Fold

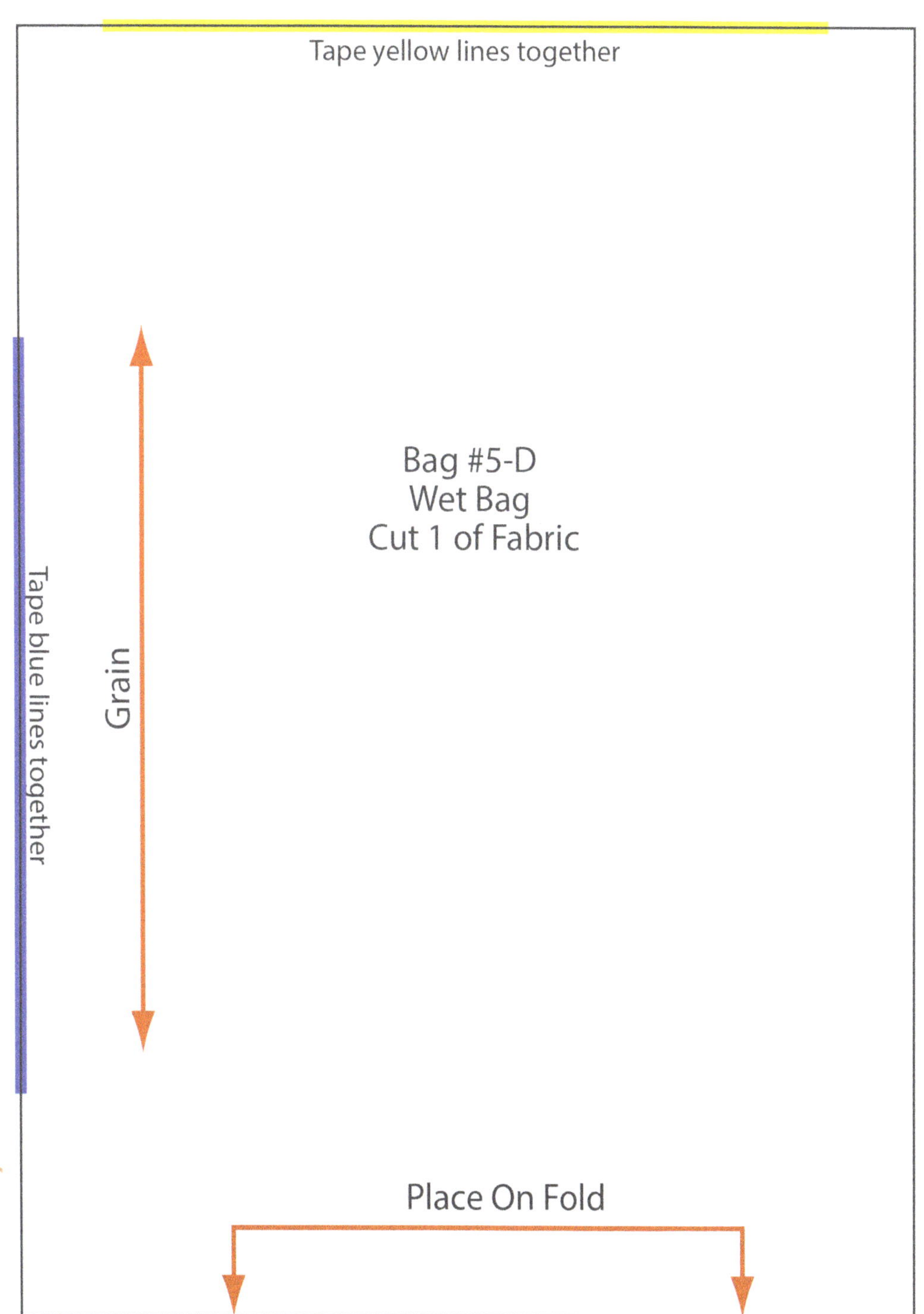
Tape yellow lines together
Bag #5-D
Wet Bag
Cut 1 of Fabric
Grain
Tape blue lines together
Place On Fold

Snack Bag Tutorial

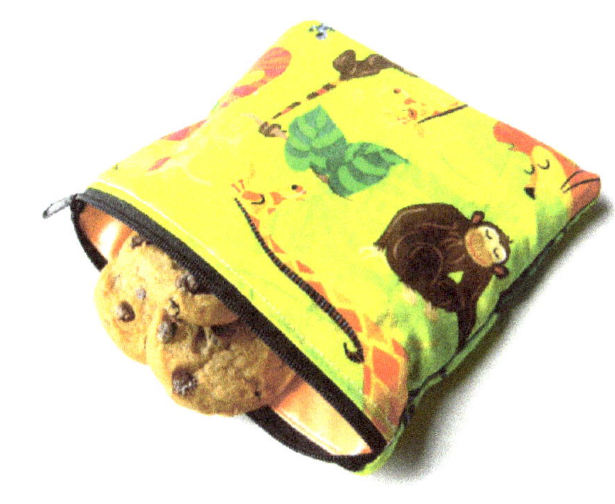

Materials:
- Cotton fabric
- Waterproof lining fabric
- Interfacing (optional)
- 1 button or snap
- Scissors
- Sewing machine with straight stitch
- Tape
- Iron
- Pins
- Thread
- 6.5"/16.5cm Zipper for Snack Bags, 7.5"/19cm Zipper for Sandwich Bag, or 10.5"/27cm Zipper for Wet Bag.

This tutorial uses Snack Size Pattern #2 and Wrist Strap #4. The same instructions can

Step 1

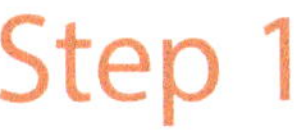

- Cut out the patterns and tape together matching color lines where necessary.

- You may want to wrap the paper wrist strap around your wrist to see if it needs to be lengthened or shortened (remember to allow for 1/4" or 6mm seam allowance at each end).

Step 2

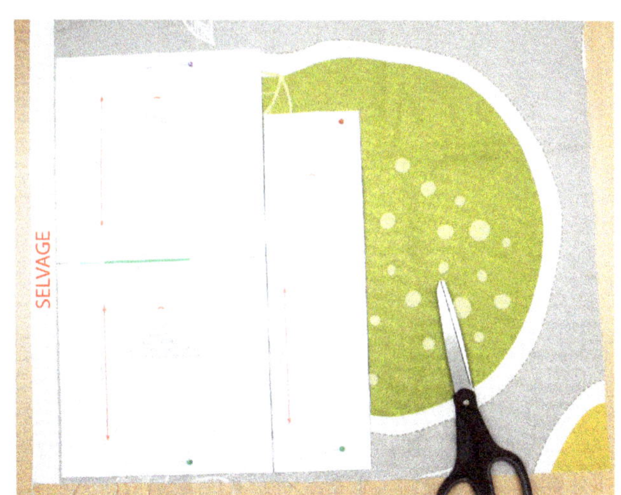

Position the pattern on the fabric so the grain line runs parallel to the grain or selvage of the fabric. (If you have directional fabric as shown in photo below with a clear top and bottom to the design place the grain line parallel to the design).

Step 3

Cut waterproof fabric and optional interfacing using the same method.

Step 4

Make the strap.

Iron or sew the optional interfacing onto the strap according to the manufacturer's instructions.

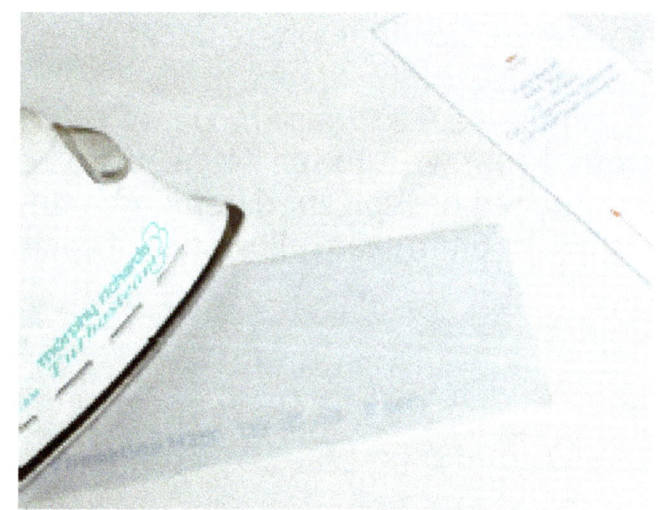

Fold strap in half one time and press with iron to create a crease.

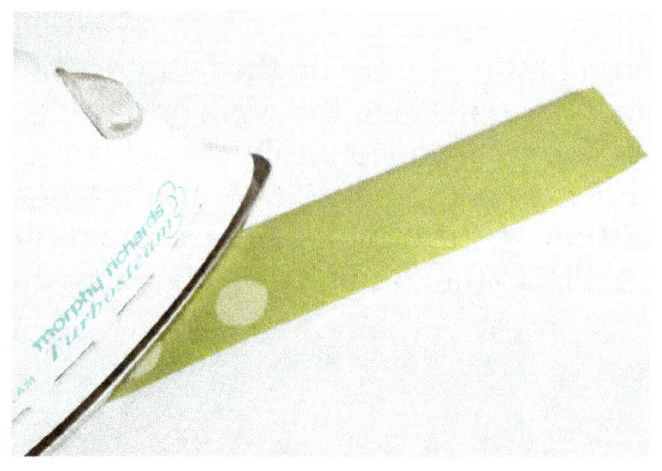

Fold both edges towards the middle crease and press.

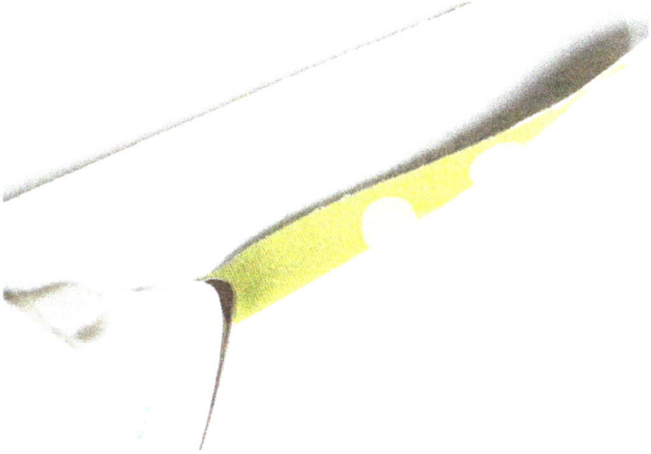

Fold strap in half again and press.

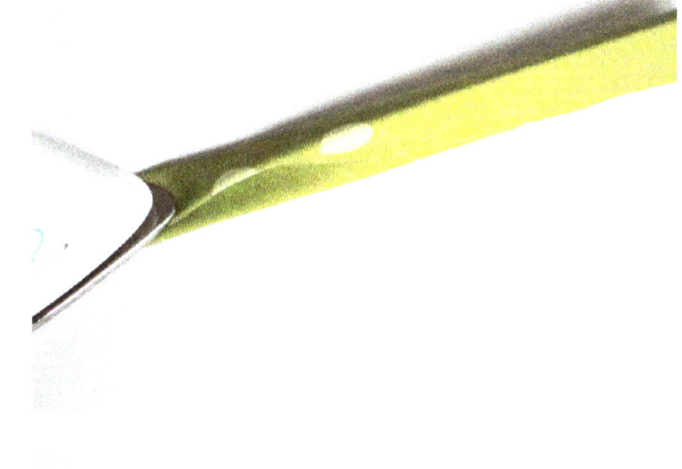

Fold edges of one end of the strap at a 45 degree angle towards the center and press.

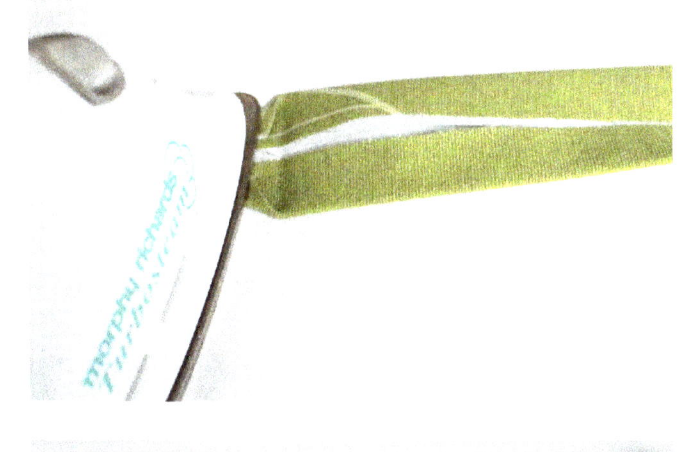

Fold a 1/4″ or 6mm hem and press.

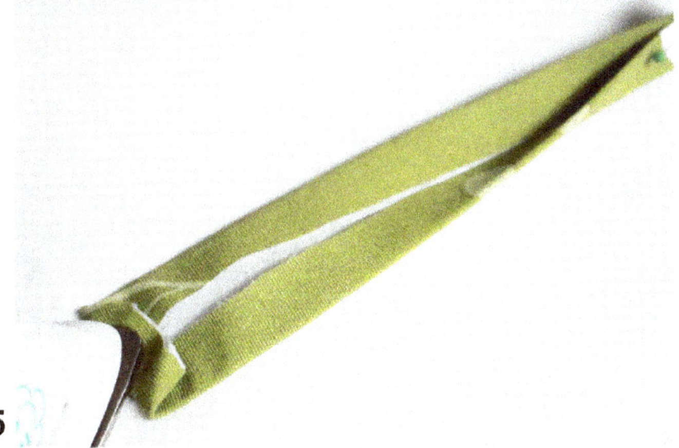

Trim away some of the excess within the hem.

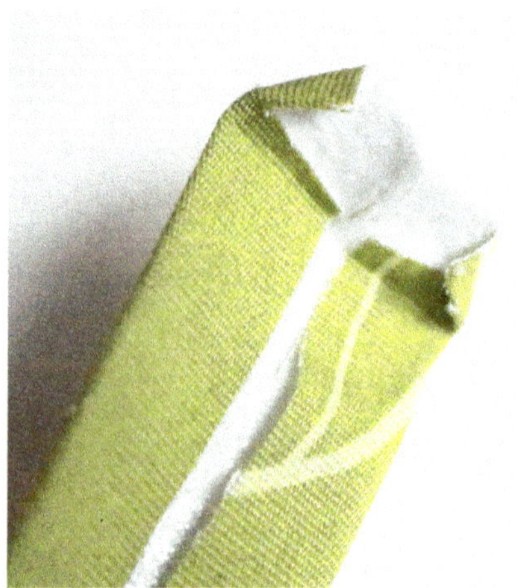

Top stitch all the way around the strap.

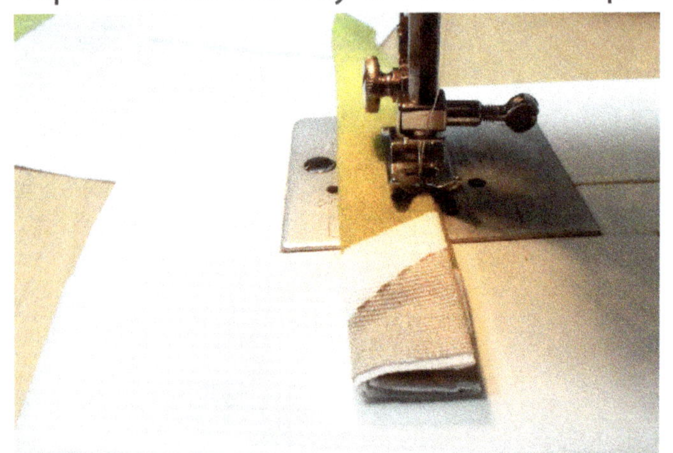

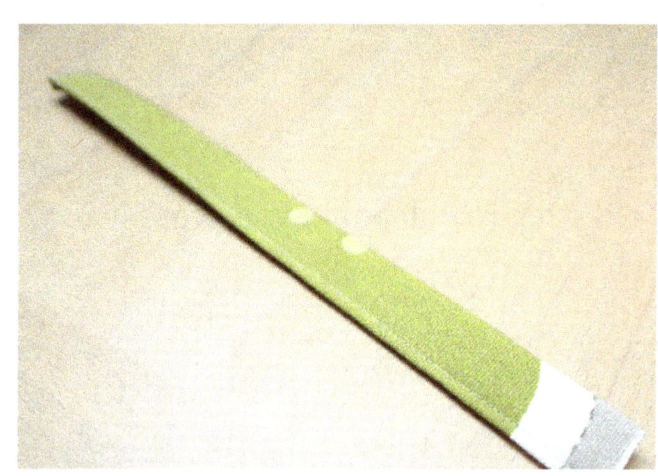

Step 5

- Position the zipper so it is closed, the zipper slider is towards the top and the teeth are facing down.

- Place the outer fabric and waterproof fabric right sides together with the zipper in between making sure the zipper teeth are facing towards the outer fabric. Pin in place. (The right side of the waterproof fabric should be the wipeable waterproof side).

- Use a zipper foot on the sewing machine and stitch 1/8" or 3mm away from the teeth.

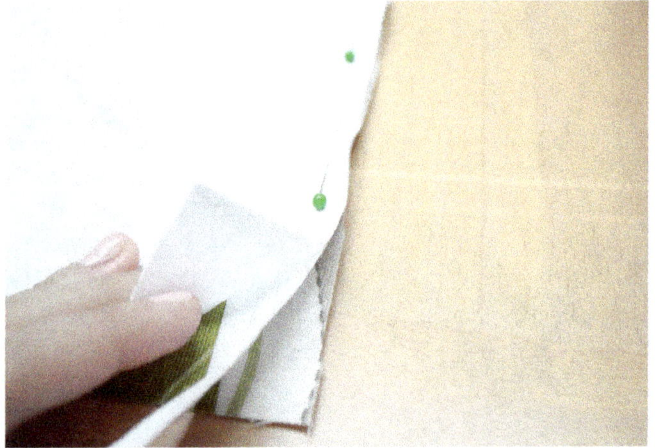

Step 6

Flip both fabrics so wrong sides are together and top stitch along the seam near the zipper teeth.

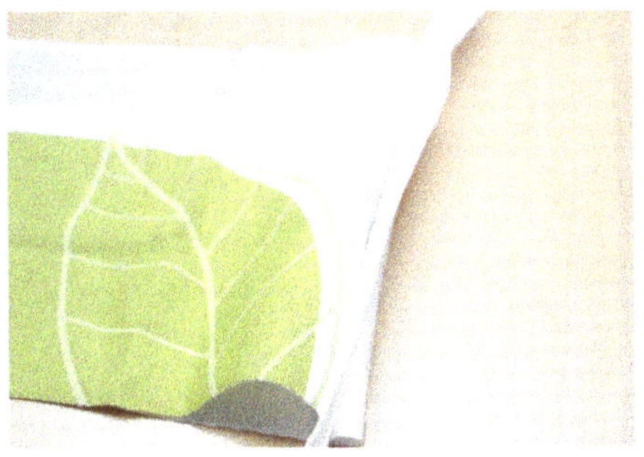
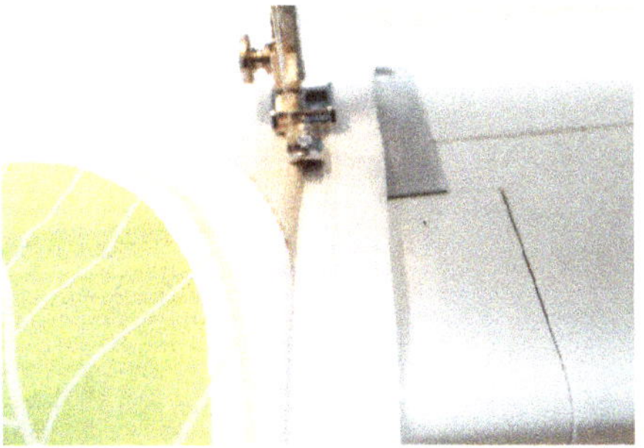
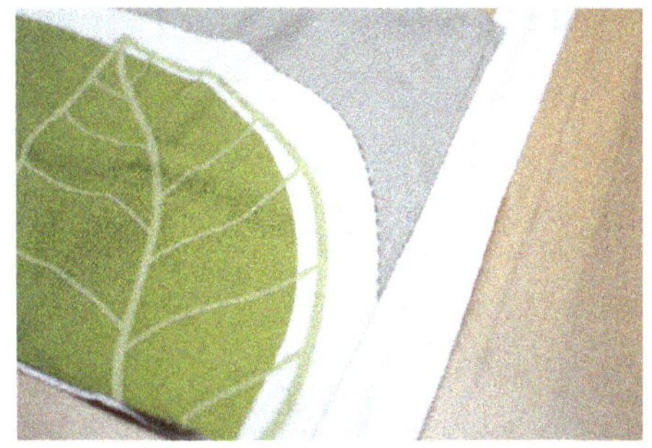

Step 7

Fold the loose end of each fabric towards the zipper so the right sides are facing together. Line up with the edge of the zipper making sure the zipper is between both fabrics and the teeth are facing up. Pin all three layers together.

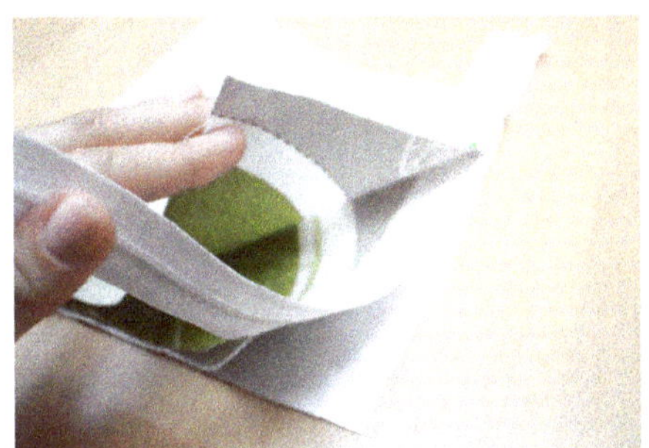

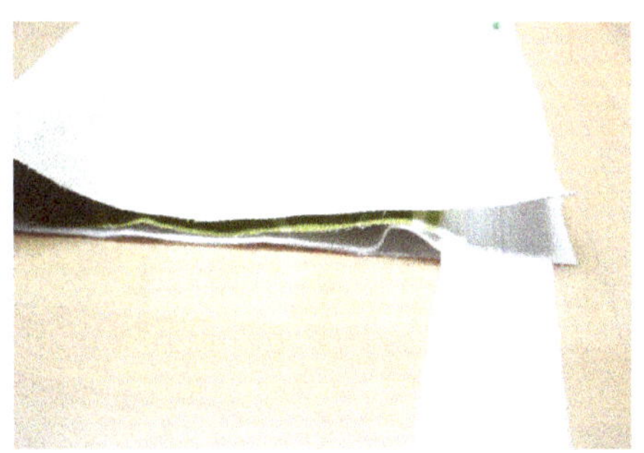

Step 8

Sew the three layers together leaving a 2″- 3″ or 5cm - 8cm gap in the center. Stretch the outer layer just a bit while sewing which will help when closing this gap later.

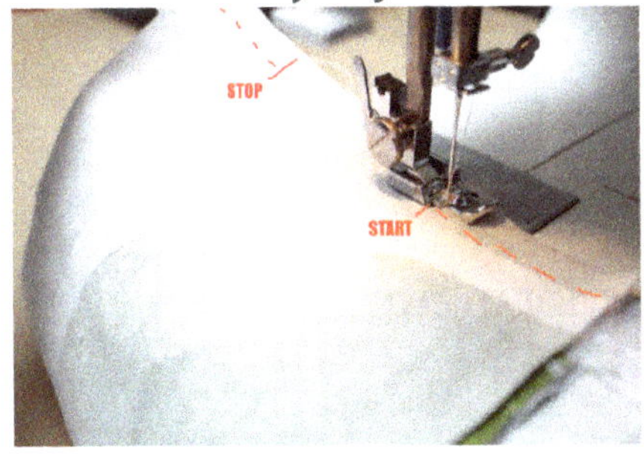

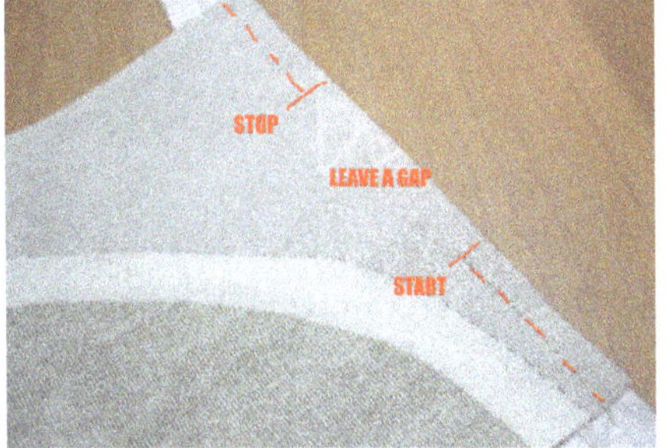

Step 9

With the outer fabric side facing up and the zipper end towards the top sew down the side of the bag through all layers. Carefully and slowly sew over the zipper to be sure not to break the needle.

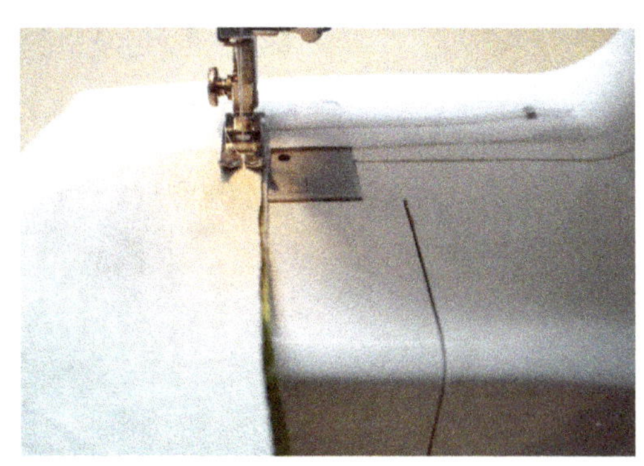

Step 10

Open the zipper and place the wrist strap between the two outer fabric layers on the remaining open side of the bag. Pin in place. Pin the side together making sure to position the open zipper teeth as close together as possible. Sew down the side of the bag.

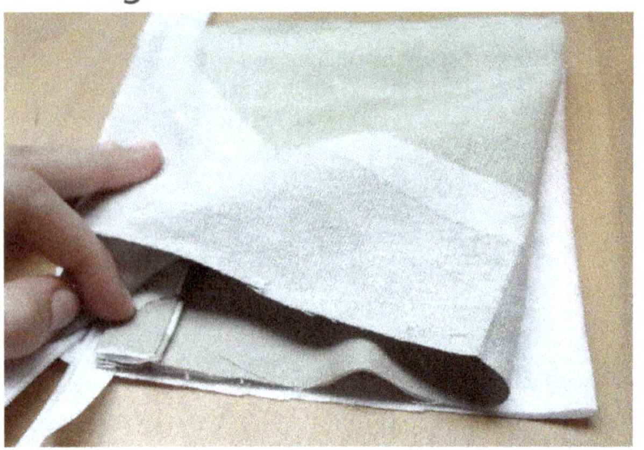

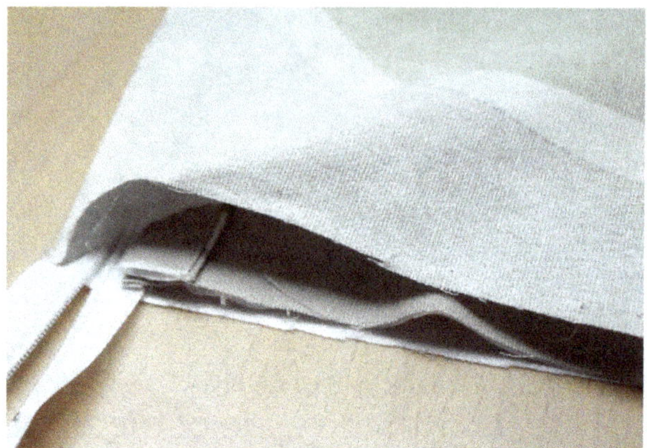

Step 11

Trim the four corners and cut off the excess zipper.

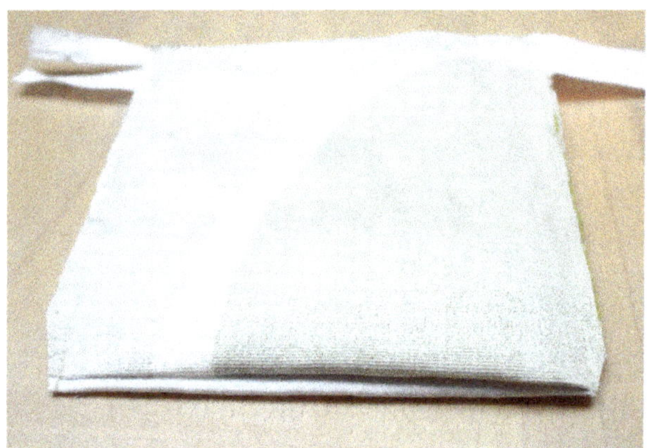

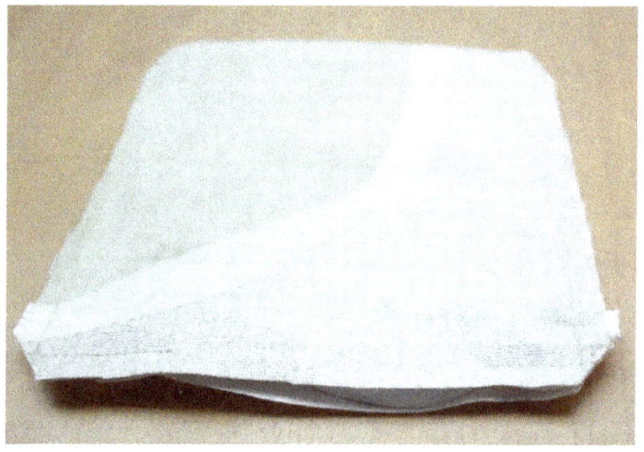

Step 12

Pull the wrist strap through the opening left at the top and turn the whole bag through. Make sure the outer fabric is ouside and the waterproof fabric is inside.

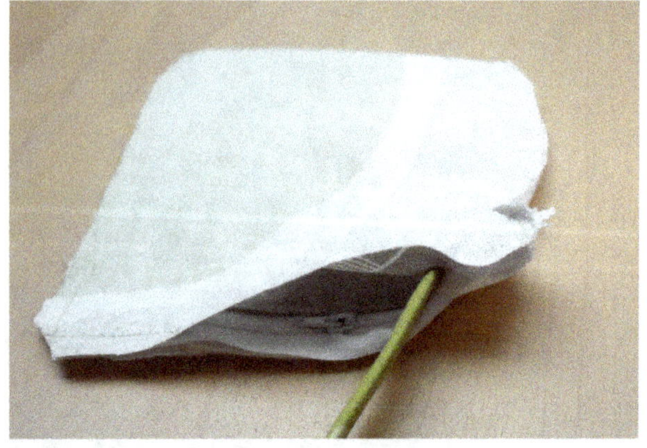

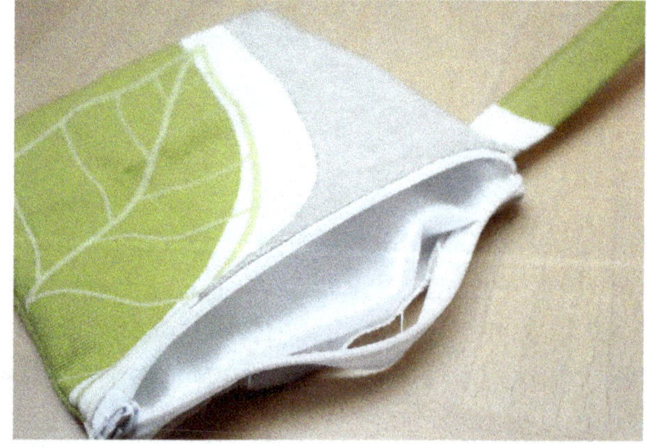

Step 13

Fold over the hem of the gap on both outer layer and waterproof layer and pin with the zipper in between.

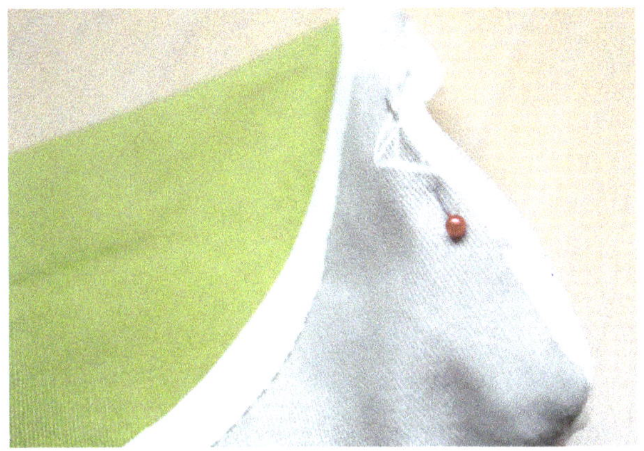

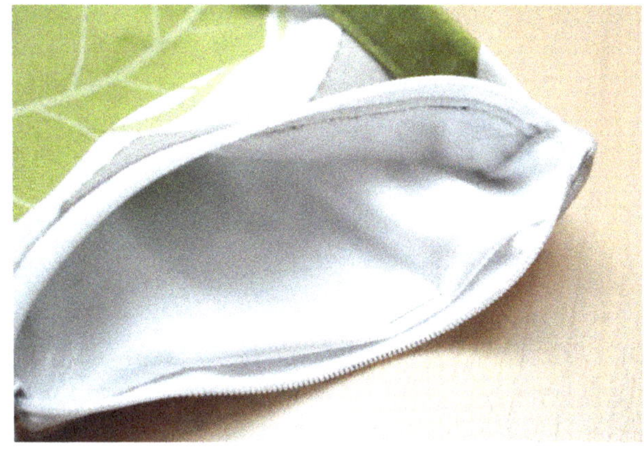

Step 14

Top stitch over the gap through all three layers.

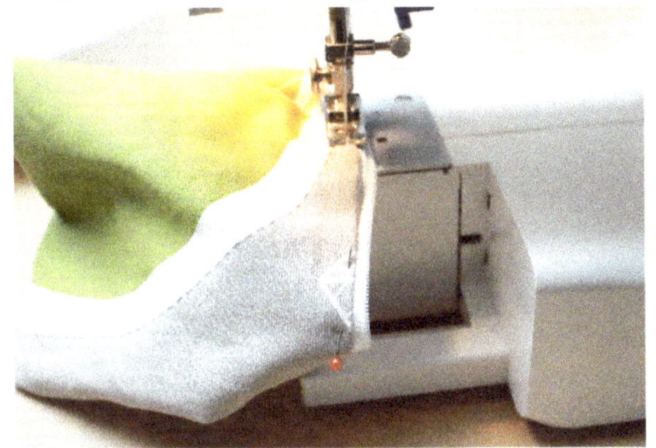

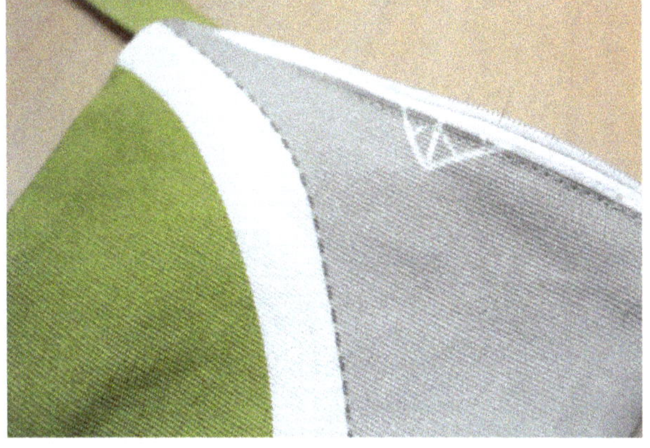

Step 15

Finish the wrist strap by adding a closure such as a button or snap.

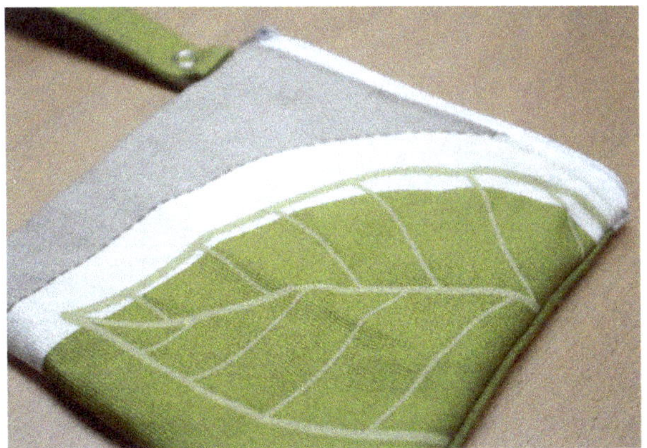

www.ingramcontent.com/pod-product-compliance
Lightning Source LLC
LaVergne TN
LVHW081409110826
845149LV00010B/1676